RENEWING ASSURANCES: STRENGTHENING U.S.-TAIWAN TIES

HEARING

BEFORE THE

SUBCOMMITTEE ON ASIA AND THE PACIFIC

OF THE

COMMITTEE ON FOREIGN AFFAIRS
HOUSE OF REPRESENTATIVES

ONE HUNDRED FIFTEENTH CONGRESS

FIRST SESSION

JUNE 15, 2017

Serial No. 115–43

Printed for the use of the Committee on Foreign Affairs

Available via the World Wide Web: http://www.foreignaffairs.house.gov/ or
http://www.gpo.gov/fdsys/

U.S. GOVERNMENT PUBLISHING OFFICE

25–846PDF   WASHINGTON : 2017

COMMITTEE ON FOREIGN AFFAIRS

EDWARD R. ROYCE, California, *Chairman*

CHRISTOPHER H. SMITH, New Jersey
ILEANA ROS-LEHTINEN, Florida
DANA ROHRABACHER, California
STEVE CHABOT, Ohio
JOE WILSON, South Carolina
MICHAEL T. McCAUL, Texas
TED POE, Texas
DARRELL E. ISSA, California
TOM MARINO, Pennsylvania
JEFF DUNCAN, South Carolina
MO BROOKS, Alabama
PAUL COOK, California
SCOTT PERRY, Pennsylvania
RON DeSANTIS, Florida
MARK MEADOWS, North Carolina
TED S. YOHO, Florida
ADAM KINZINGER, Illinois
LEE M. ZELDIN, New York
DANIEL M. DONOVAN, JR., New York
F. JAMES SENSENBRENNER, JR.,
 Wisconsin
ANN WAGNER, Missouri
BRIAN J. MAST, Florida
FRANCIS ROONEY, Florida
BRIAN K. FITZPATRICK, Pennsylvania
THOMAS A. GARRETT, JR., Virginia

ELIOT L. ENGEL, New York
BRAD SHERMAN, California
GREGORY W. MEEKS, New York
ALBIO SIRES, New Jersey
GERALD E. CONNOLLY, Virginia
THEODORE E. DEUTCH, Florida
KAREN BASS, California
WILLIAM R. KEATING, Massachusetts
DAVID N. CICILLINE, Rhode Island
AMI BERA, California
LOIS FRANKEL, Florida
TULSI GABBARD, Hawaii
JOAQUIN CASTRO, Texas
ROBIN L. KELLY, Illinois
BRENDAN F. BOYLE, Pennsylvania
DINA TITUS, Nevada
NORMA J. TORRES, California
BRADLEY SCOTT SCHNEIDER, Illinois
THOMAS R. SUOZZI, New York
ADRIANO ESPAILLAT, New York
TED LIEU, California

AMY PORTER, *Chief of Staff*   THOMAS SHEEHY, *Staff Director*
JASON STEINBAUM, *Democratic Staff Director*

———

SUBCOMMITTEE ON ASIA AND THE PACIFIC

TED S. YOHO, Florida, *Chairman*

DANA ROHRABACHER, California
STEVE CHABOT, Ohio
TOM MARINO, Pennsylvania
MO BROOKS, Alabama
SCOTT PERRY, Pennsylvania
ADAM KINZINGER, Illinois
ANN WAGNER, Missouri

BRAD SHERMAN, California
AMI BERA, California
DINA TITUS, Nevada
GERALD E. CONNOLLY, Virginia
THEODORE E. DEUTCH, Florida
TULSI GABBARD, Hawaii

CONTENTS

Page

WITNESSES

LETTERS, STATEMENTS, ETC., SUBMITTED FOR THE HEARING

APPENDIX

RENEWING ASSURANCES: STRENGTHENING U.S.-TAIWAN TIES

THURSDAY, JUNE 15, 2017

House of Representatives,
Subcommittee on Asia and the Pacific,
Committee on Foreign Affairs,
Washington, DC.

The subcommittee met, pursuant to notice, at 2:45 p.m., in room 2200 Rayburn House Office Building, Hon. Ted Yoho (chairman of the subcommittee) presiding.

Mr. YOHO. The subcommittee will come to order. For those of you that were present and you saw Republicans and Democrats on both sides, that wasn't dysfunction. That was to show you the Foreign Affairs Committee is very well united and that was done purposely, right?

The subcommittee will come to order. Members present will be permitted to submit written statements to be included in the official hearing record. Without objection, the hearing record will remain open for 5 calendar days to allow statements, questions, and extraneous material for the record subject to length, limitations, and the rules.

Good afternoon. Taiwan has received significant attention in Congress since last year—excuse me—has not received significant attention in Congress since last year. At that time, the focus was on the campaign and later the victory of President Tsai Ing-wen, and the mood was optimistic and celebratory.

Since that time, unfortunately, Taiwan's international outlook has become increasingly cloudy. Just this week, Panama severed diplomatic ties with Taiwan and recognized the People's Republic of China, a gut-wrenching loss for Taiwan's dwindling diplomatic recognition. Last month, the PRC blocked Taiwan's delegation from attending the World Health Assembly in Geneva, the annual gathering of the World Health Organization, despite the fact that Taiwan has regularly attended the summit and has been an international force for good in the health space. It is not only Taiwan's loss, but the world's as diseases know no borders.

Since President Tsai's election, the PRC has escalated a global campaign to squeeze Taiwan's international recognition out of existence. Taiwan's security situation is being challenged alongside its diplomatic presence. The PRC has undertaken unprecedented military provocations around Taiwan in recent months. In November of last year, China flew aircraft around the perimeter of Taiwan's Air Defense Identification Zone for the first time. In January, the PRC sailed the Liaoning, its first aircraft carrier, through the Taiwan Straits.

These actions, the PRC's increasing global military ambition, and its belligerence in the East and South China Seas have contributed to an environment of instability. However, the United States has not completed an arms sale to Taiwan since 2015, though the Taiwan Relations Act requires the United States to offer the necessary equipment for Taiwan's self-defenses capabilities.

Successive administrations have shown a lack of resolve in executing our defense commitments to Taiwan, emboldening the PRC which remains uncommitted to a peaceful resolution of Taiwan's status. Our most recent arms sales was in 2015, and the prior sales were years apart. Since 2008, sales have been delayed so that they can be bundled together and their timing can be manipulated. The arms sales process has become a political calculation designed to minimize friction with the PRC. Not only does this concede to Beijing a degree of influence over our arms sales process, it seems to contravene President Reagan's assurance that the PRC would not be consulted on arms sales to Taiwan.

Economic pressure on Taiwan is increasing as well. Taiwan has long been a developed, high-tech economy, and is especially dependent on international trade for its prosperity and economic growth. But the PRC's massive and growing economic clout grants it the ability to exclude Taiwan from trade agreements and to use economic pressure to change other nations' policies toward Taiwan.

It is astonishing to think that the backwards, isolated PRC of 1979 could someday bring this level of diplomatic, security, and economic pressure to bear. This geopolitical reality that was held when we established our One China Policy has changed. The People's Republic of China is no longer the third party to a great power competition between the United States and the Soviet Union. It has become a challenger, seeking to attain great power status for itself by overturning a peaceful unipolar order.

Despite this, our One China Policy has remained virtually unchanged since 1979. It is important for Congress to consider whether our policies are still serving us well and how we might improve them. In particular, renewing our assurances to Taiwan to continue and steadfast U.S. support is especially important.

We have convened this hearing today to work toward these goals, and I thank the witnesses and I thank my colleagues for joining me today to help strengthen U.S.-Taiwan ties. And, without objection, the witness' written statement will be entered into the hearing, and I now turn to the ranking member for any remarks he may have.

[The prepared statement of Mr. Yoho follows:]

Opening Statement of the Honorable **Ted Yoho (R-FL), Chairman**
House Foreign Affairs Subcommittee on Asia and the Pacific Hearing:
"Renewing Assurances: Strengthening U.S.-Taiwan Ties"
June 15, 2017

(As prepared for delivery)

Good afternoon. Taiwan has not received significant attention in Congress since last year. At that time, the focus was on the campaign and later the victory of President Tsai Ing-wen, and the mood was optimistic and celebratory. Since that time, unfortunately, Taiwan's international outlook has become increasingly cloudy.

Diplomatic Pressure and International Space

Just this week, Panama severed diplomatic ties with Taiwan and recognized the People's Republic of China, a gut wrenching loss for Taiwan's dwindling diplomatic recognition. Last month, the PRC blocked Taiwan's delegation from attending the World Health Assembly in Geneva, the annual gathering of the World Health Organization, despite the fact that Taiwan has regularly attended the summit and has been an international force for good in the health space. It is not only Taiwan's loss, but the world's as diseases know no borders.

Since President Tsai's election, the PRC has escalated a global campaign to squeeze Taiwan's international recognition out of existence.

Security and Economic Environment

Taiwan's security situation is being challenged alongside its diplomatic presence. The PRC has undertaken unprecedented military provocations around Taiwan in recent months. In November of last year, China flew aircraft around the perimeter of Taiwan's Air Defense Identification Zone for the first time. In January, the PRC sailed the Liaoning, its first aircraft carrier, through the Taiwan Strait.

These actions, the PRC's increasingly global military ambitions, and its belligerence in the East and South China Seas have contributed to an environment of instability. However, the United States has *not* completed an arms sale to Taiwan since 2015, though the Taiwan Relations Act requires the United States to offer the necessary equipment for Taiwan's self-defense capability.

Successive administrations have shown a lack of resolve in executing our defense commitments to Taiwan, emboldening the PRC, which remains uncommitted to a peaceful resolution of Taiwan's status. Our most recent arms sale was in 2015, and the prior sales were years apart. Since 2008, sales have been delayed so that they can be bundled together and their timing can be manipulated.

The arms sales process has become a political calculation designed to minimize friction with the PRC. Not only does this concede to Beijing a degree of influence over our arms sales process, it seems to contravene President Reagan's assurance that the PRC would not be consulted on arms sales to Taiwan.

Economic pressure on Taiwan is increasing as well. Taiwan has long been a developed, high-tech economy, and is especially dependent on international trade for its prosperity and economic growth. But the PRC's massive and growing economic clout grants it the ability to exclude Taiwan from trade agreements, and to use economic pressure to change other nations' policies towards Taiwan. It is astonishing to think that the backwards, isolated PRC of 1979 could someday bring this level of diplomatic, security, and economic pressure to bear.

The Future of U.S. Policy for Taiwan

The geopolitical reality that held when we established our "One China" policy has changed. The People's Republic of China is no longer the third party to a great power competition between the United States and the Soviet Union. It has become a challenger, seeking to attain great power status for itself by overturning a peaceful unipolar order.

Despite this, our "One China" policy has remained virtually unchanged since 1979. It is important for Congress to consider whether our policies are still serving us well, and how we might improve them. In particular, renewing our assurances to Taiwan of continued and steadfast U.S. support is especially important. We've convened this hearing today to work towards these goals, and I thank the witnesses and my colleagues for joining me today to help strengthen U.S.-Taiwan ties.

Mr. SHERMAN. Thank you, Mr. Chairman, for holding this hearing. I was impressed when I met President Tsai when she was in the opposition when we met in Taipei in 2015, and even more impressed when she visited the United States in 2016 and came to my district. Now she is the only female President in the region.

The United States has a strong interest in supporting the people of Taiwan and those interests are enshrined in the Taiwan Relations Act and we need to abide by the six assurances. Our clear message should be that the United States does believe in the power of dialogue, but we unequivocally support the right of the people of Taiwan to determine their own government through elections.

Taiwan should not be used as a bargaining chip. Our relationships with China are important, their dealings with North Korea are important, but we need to stand by the Taiwan Relations Act for many reasons, including that Taiwan is a democratic partner.

Freedom House recently upgraded its appraisal of Taiwan's democracy from 1.5 up to 1, which is their highest rating, noting not only the success of the 2016 elections, but also increased freedom in the area of press and academic freedom. Taiwan respects human rights, LGBT rights, et cetera. Taiwan is a partner of ours in intelligence and in cybersecurity, and it is miles ahead of China when it comes to protecting intellectual property.

The Taiwan Travel Act is important. We should be upgrading, certainly not downgrading, our relationship with Taiwan. Taiwan is a country of 23 million people. At many times we have sold them billions of dollars in arms, but, surprisingly, in spite of that we do not allow Taiwanese officials to travel to the United States in any official capacity. Instead, we have this ruse where they can only come if they are refueling to go to some Latin American country of far less interest to the Taiwanese officials than the United States is, and stay in our country for a day or two during that refueling process.

This is incredibly inconvenient to my colleagues. It is, however, very convenient for me since the tradition of not only this but prior Taiwanese Presidents is that when they land in Los Angeles they come immediately to a Taiwanese hotel in my district. So I am the only member perhaps that should oppose the Taiwan Travel Act, but I do indeed support it. That is why I joined with our colleague, Steve Chabot, introducing it and it of course expresses the sense of Congress that it should be U.S. policy to have governmental leaders of Taiwan free to visit the United States.

The U.S. needs to be an advocate for Taiwanese participation in international relations whether that be Interpol, whether that be the World Health Assembly. China's efforts to degrade Taiwan's participation in these international organizations is not just outrageous for the 23 million people who should be represented in these organizations, it is bad for the entire world. The only beneficiaries are diseases and international criminals.

Taiwan is part of the world and its involvement in these organizations are necessary for Interpol, the World Health Assembly, the WHO to achieve its objectives, their various objectives. As to Lee Ming-Che, who has been arrested in China for so-called activities endangering national security, she has not received visitation rights. His condition is questionable and this is unacceptable.

We look forward to Taiwan diversifying its trade and economic relationships, not only deepening them with the United States but also other countries so it is not dependent on China. We note the new Southbound Policy to engage with South and Southeast Asia. As far as our own relationship with Taiwan, we are talking about $85 billion in trade. We do have a trade deficit but it is a modest one given the size of the relationship. That is contrasted with the highly lopsided, almost metastasized relationship we have with China, and I look forward to seeing what we can do to even, to make that trade deficit even smaller. With that I yield back.

Mr. YOHO. Thank you, Mr. Sherman. And we had the distinct pleasure, she stopped in Miami. President Tsai stopped there to have dinner with us as she was going to refuel with you, so it was a great moment.

Mr. SHERMAN. Is that your opposition to the act?

Mr. YOHO. That was bipartisanship.

Mr. SHERMAN. Bipartisan opposition.

Mr. YOHO. We have been joined by the chairman of the full committee, Mr. Royce, for a statement.

Mr. ROYCE. Well, thank you, Chairman Yoho. I appreciate that and let me just mention also that I appreciate you having this hearing. I appreciate the markup that preceded this on the Taiwan Travel Act. I am also a cosponsor of that legislation. I think by encouraging more visits between the two governments, including at the highest levels, we are going to further strengthen the critical U.S.-Taiwan partnership. I think we share certain commitments—one of them is democracy, another is human rights, the rule of law—and it is really these values that serve as the bedrock of this partnership.

And as these members have accompanied me, I will just mention also that every year I lead a large bipartisan delegation to Taiwan to highlight the broad and steadfast relationship that the U.S. has with Taiwan, and this was made possible by the Taiwan Relations Act of 1979. Taiwan is facing new challenges as a result of changes in cross-strait and global dynamics as well, and it is more important than ever to reassure Taiwan of the U.S. commitment to the relationship.

Unfortunately, just this week, under pressure and with inducements from Beijing, Panama broke off decades of diplomatic relations with Taiwan and switched diplomatic recognition to the People's Republic of China. This decision from Panamanian President Varela came after Taiwan has, according to media reports, provided $20 million per year in foreign aid to Panama, on average. I would hope that Panama, and all nations, would act to include Taiwan in international organizations.

I found it particularly concerning that Taiwan was excluded from this year's World Health Assembly, especially when we consider that wherever we go internationally after a disaster we see Taiwanese physicians, doctors, and civil society show up to assist. Taiwan has contributed to international efforts obviously to improve global health with financial and technical assistance, and the Ebola case would just be one of many, many that have occurred. It is for this reason that Taiwan has been invited to the World Health Assembly for the past 8 years. Taiwan's exclusion this year only hurts global health, as our colleague Congressman Brad Sherman has said. There should have been no question about Taiwan's participation.

I am a strong advocate for strengthening Taiwan's economic links to the United States and across Asia. Taiwan, as we all know, is the tenth largest goods trading partner, and the seventh largest market for our farmers and ranchers. Taiwanese companies invest substantially here. Taiwanese companies have pledged $34 billion in investments into the U.S. in 2017, and with our shared values of democracy and open markets it is vital that we continue to grow this economic partnership. Chairman Yoho understands this and has taken the lead on this issue by authoring legislation to encourage a deeper trade relationship between the U.S. and Taiwan, and I am a cosponsor and supporter of those efforts.

Finally, one of the key provisions of the Taiwan Relations Act was the commitment from the United States to provide Taiwan with defensive arms. I remain concerned about successive administrations' delays in our arms sales notification for Taiwan. I think this needlessly draws out the arms sales process. I hope to see regular notifications in the future and I look forward to the announcement of new sales this year.

Again I thank Chairman Yoho, and I am looking forward to the witness' testimony.

Mr. YOHO. Chairman Royce, thank you for being here. It is an honor to have you here. At this moment we are thankful today to be joined by Mr. Rupert Hammond-Chambers.

Mr. Chabot, did you have something you want to add?

Mr. CHABOT. If the chair, because I am more than happy——

Mr. YOHO. No, go ahead, my oversight.

Mr. CHABOT. I was just going to say I will associate myself with the chairman's comments and leave it there so that we can move on to the witnesses.

Mr. YOHO. Thank you, sir. We are joined today by Mr. Rupert Hammond-Chambers, president of the U.S.-Taiwan Business Council; Mr. Dan Blumenthal, director of the Asian Studies and a resident fellow at the American Enterprise Institute; and Mr. Russell Hsiao, executive director of the Global Taiwan Institute. We thank the panel for joining us today and share their experience and expertise and we look forward to that. You will have approximately 5 minutes to give your opening statement. The green light will come on, and then don't forget to hit the button to turn your mike on. Mr. Chambers, we will start with you. Thank you.

STATEMENT OF MR. RUPERT J. HAMMOND-CHAMBERS, PRESIDENT, U.S.-TAIWAN BUSINESS COUNCIL

Mr. HAMMOND-CHAMBERS. Thank you, Mr. Chairman and Mr. Chairman, members of the committee, it is an honor to be with you today. Taiwan remains a critical global partner for the United States. As noted, it is in fact our tenth largest trading partner which is extraordinary when you consider the island has very little in the way of natural resources and 23 million people living on a relatively small island. The economy surpasses $447 billion in annual GDP and its currency reserves now surpass $440 billion.

By any measure, Taiwan is a poster-child example of the success of post-World War II U.S. foreign policy and its support for the building of flourishing free market democracies. Taiwan is worthy of significant investment by the United States, not just to support the island but as a representation of America's sustained commitment to the region. Since 2005, however, the U.S.-Taiwan relationship has seen significant distress. And again, as noted successive administrations have downgraded the bar of support for the island in the face of an increasingly aggressive and hegemonic People's Republic of China. The PRC campaign to undermine support for Taiwan continues apace, with a focus on linking China's behavior on non-Taiwan matters, such as North Korea, to the willingness of the U.S. to curb its support for Taiwan in areas critical to Taiwan's ongoing peace and security such as arms sales and expanded trade relations.

As the PRC's economic and military power grows, the United States is increasingly challenged to assess whether it is willing to maintain its ongoing interest with Taiwan or if it will abdicate that leadership role in the hopes of moderating China's behavior in other areas of national interest. The U.S.-Taiwan Business Council believes that U.S. trade with Taiwan is mutually beneficial, despite the consistent trade deficit in goods in favor of Taiwan that has persisted over the last 30 years.

Taiwan plays a tremendously important role both as a market for U.S.-made goods, as a manufacturing and innovation partner for U.S. businesses. You only need to look at your iPhone as an example of the importance and day-to-day partnership that the U.S. has with Taiwan. Goods and services trade with Taiwan along with extensive investments by Taiwan businesses in the U.S. promotes economic growth here and supports U.S. jobs across the country and in many industries. The U.S.-Taiwan Business Council also believes that Taiwan is a well-placed partner with this administration and this Congress in exploring and partnering on new bilateral trade initiatives including the possibility of signing a fair trade agreement.

The Taiwan Relations Act clearly states that the U.S. will remain obligated to provide Taiwan with arms of a defensive character as noted already in formal comments.

The U.S. is Taiwan's primary military partner and retains a close material relationship with the island that covers not only arms sales, but also cooperation on cyber intelligence, training, maintenance, and logistics. Past U.S. policy, particularly under the Obama administration, focused significant efforts on the expansion of training and exchanges. While it goes mostly unseen, it does have a material impact on the island's defense.

In instances where U.S. commitments to Taiwan's defense are discreetly carried out, there has been stability and ingenuity in expanding cooperation. However, where the commitment is overt, such as with arms sales under the Taiwan Relations Act, there has been significant regression particularly since 2011. As of June 15, 2017, we have seen only a single sale of arms to Taiwan, in 2015, since as far back as September the 21, 2011. A closer inspection of the trend lines shows a material U.S. commitment in free fall. The Trump administration has been handed a challenge to assess and deliver on a new range of commitments for Taiwan's national defense such as new fighters and diesel-electric submarines.

U.S. strategic interests in the Asia-Pacific remain inexorably intertwined with our support for Taiwan's economy and national security. However, this aspirational goal is being undermined by an orchestrated and coercive PRC policy to weaken support for Taiwan and to restrict Taiwan's self-determination.

If the U.S. continues to rhetorically say the right things but materially fails to act, then Taiwan risks being further marginalized globally and will be forced to interact with China from a weak position. This is inherently destabilizing. The present trajectory could lead to a crisis in the Taiwan Strait triggered by China's determination that the overall trilateral balance has tipped squarely in its favor and that China would then act accordingly. Thank you very much.

[The prepared statement of Mr. Hammond-Chambers follows:]

Renewing Assurances: Strengthening U.S.-Taiwan Ties

Subcommittee on Asia and the Pacific
House Foreign Affairs Committee

June 15, 2017

Rupert Hammond-Chambers
President
US-Taiwan Business Council

Renewing Assurances: Strengthening U.S.-Taiwan Ties

June 15, 2017

Table of Contents

Renewing Assurances: Strengthening U.S.-Taiwan Ties

June 15, 2017

Introduction

Taiwan remains a critical global partner for the United States. It is currently our 10th largest trading partner, ahead of India and other strategically important countries, and it serves as a critical node in the defense and security architecture of the U.S. across Asia.

Taiwan's population of 23.5 million people is roughly the same as Australia, but the island sits on a land mass equivalent to 0.47% of that of Australia. In the absence of any significant natural resources, other than its people, Taiwan has built an economy surpassing US$474 billion in annual GDP, and foreign currency reserves surpassing US$440 billion. Taiwan was still receiving U.S. foreign aid in the early 1950s, but has since flourished as it opened its markets and its political system.

By any measure, Taiwan is a poster-child example of the success of post-World War II U.S. foreign policy and its support for the building of flourishing free market democracies. Taiwan is worthy of significant investment by the United States, not just to support the island but as a representation of America's sustained commitment to the region.

In April 1979, the U.S. Congress passed the Taiwan Relations Act (TRA), embedding U.S. policy towards Taiwan into law and providing the framework for future support. Meanwhile, it also set important boundaries for behavior by the People's Republic of China (PRC) after the U.S. switch in diplomatic recognition earlier that year.

Since 2005, however, the U.S.-Taiwan relationship has been on a steady decline. Successive Republican and Democratic administrations have downgraded the bar of support for the island in the face of an increasingly aggressive and hegemonic PRC.

The PRC campaign to undermine support for Taiwan continues apace, with a focus on linking China's behavior on non-Taiwan matters – such as North Korea – to the willingness of the U.S. to curb its support for Taiwan in areas critical to Taiwan's ongoing welfare, such as arms sales and expanded trade relations.

As the PRC's economic and military power grows, the United States is increasingly challenged to assess whether it is willing to maintain its ongoing interest with Taiwan or if it will abdicate that leadership role in the hopes of moderating China's behavior in other areas of national interest.

Trade & Economic Ties

The U.S. is Taiwan's second largest trading partner behind only China, and the two have approximately US$66 billion in annual two-way trade. A strong and economically prosperous Taiwan is in the interests of the Unites States, and should be a core pillar of American support for the island.

The US-Taiwan Business Council (USTBC) believes that U.S. trade with Taiwan is mutually beneficial, despite the consistent trade deficit in goods in favor of Taiwan that has persisted for the last 30 years. Taiwan plays a tremendously important role both as a market for U.S.-made goods and as a manufacturing and innovation partner for U.S. businesses. Goods and services trade with Taiwan – along with extensive investments by Taiwan businesses in the U.S. – generally promotes economic growth in the United States and supports U.S. jobs across the country and in many industries. USTBC also believes that Taiwan is well placed to partner with the Trump Administration in exploring and partnering on new bilateral trade initiatives, including possibly signing a Fair Trade Agreement (FTA).

Taiwan's economy has flourished, particularly since the 1980s, by positioning itself as a partner in manufacturing products with high quality and low cost. Our bilateral economic relations are primarily underpinned by Taiwan's partnership with the U.S. in the development and production of information technology (IT) products, with the intellectual property for these products typically held by a third party.

For example, Apple's primary production partner for its iPhones is Foxconn, a Taiwan company with large manufacturing investments both in China and across the globe. Its production prowess allows for Apple to produce, on a large scale, millions of devices that support its operating systems and applications. The device itself typically accounts for less than 20% of the final consumer price, with the remaining 80%+ going to the holders of the internal intellectual property. This arrangement has benefited all parties, and has created considerable wealth and productivity gains in both the U.S. and Taiwan.

However, Taiwan's economy is currently at a crossroads. The tight operating margins of such contract manufacturing has placed considerable pressure on Taiwan industry to innovate, to invest more in research and development, and for the government of Taiwan to improve the start-up environment for entrepreneurs. Taiwan's rapid pace of development has now slowed as companies have matured. In addition, the emergence of new, innovative Taiwan businesses has also slowed dramatically.

U.S. Trade Policy Towards Taiwan

U.S. trade policy toward Taiwan since 2003 has been fraught with tension over the protection of intellectual property (2003-2005), over struggles regarding beef (2007-2012), and over the current issues with pork trade. In each case, U.S. trade negotiators have chosen to sever ongoing trade links over these periods in an attempt to pressure Taiwan into making changes to its economic and trade behavior. There is also a bureaucratic reluctance to move forward on trade initiatives with Taiwan for fear that they may disrupt similar initiatives with the PRC.

The U.S. strategy – an ongoing insistence that for Taiwan to take the next step in trade ties, they must first undertake significant changes – has left U.S.-Taiwan trade ties adrift for a good portion of the past 14 years. These preconditions, however, change as Taiwan goes ahead and addresses them. USTBC is unaware of any other major U.S. trading partner being similarly treated, and regrettably U.S. exporters have been hurt by the under-realized development of this important market.

Since 2013, the U.S. has pressed Taiwan to undertake unilateral action on its pork import regime, specifically the admittance of pork containing the steroid ractopamine. Taiwan's domestic political constraints have prohibited such a

unilateral concession, and Taiwan has argued for this issue to be addressed in a broader bilateral negotiation. Importantly, Senator Chuck Grassley (R-IA) – a leading advocate for American farmers – recently changed his position from demanding that pork be addressed as a precondition for any FTA negotiations, to arguing that it should be addressed in a broader negotiation with Taiwan. His change in position removes an important impediment in the possible expansion of trade relations between the U.S. and Taiwan. However, past experience suggests that new U.S. preconditions to broader ties may now appear.

USTBC remains committed to maximizing America's commercial relations with Taiwan. While there are a number of outstanding trade issues with the island, we do not support preconditions on the path to broader ties or as an impediment to the launch of Fair Trade Agreement negotiations.

Taiwan can help this process by improving communication and cooperation through an increase in the number of visits to Washington, D.C. by Cabinet members and by sub-Cabinet officials. For many years, Taiwan's trade relationship was underpinned by constant engagement, with many senior economic officials in particular visiting Washington. Those types of visits have largely dried up, however, as both the U.S. and Taiwan became over-focused on China during the 2008-2016 timeframe. In Taiwan, the demands placed on the executive branch by the Taiwan legislature have curbed the enthusiasm of its leadership to undertake foreign travel during ongoing sessions. This is hurting the bilateral relationship, and allows for PRC messaging to dominate U.S. government considerations.

Conversely, the limits on U.S. officials traveling to Taiwan – particularly from the U.S. Department of State and U.S. Department of Defense – inhibit the ability of U.S. government officials and staff to make sound judgements on U.S. policy, and to address the constant drumbeat of China's position as it relates to Taiwan.

Importantly, Taiwan needs to better integrate itself into the Asia Pacific region's ongoing trade liberalization architecture. However, it is likely that any such effort will remain unsuccessful in the absence of U.S. leadership. Asia Pacific countries will not engage with Taiwan in FTA negotiations in the face of PRC objections, unless the U.S. offers leadership and an established framework. It is the USTBC's view that if the U.S. does launch FTA negotiations with Taiwan, we can reasonably expect Japan, Australia, India and some ASEAN countries to follow-suit.

Defense & Security Relations

Taiwan's geographic location is of significant importance to U.S. security, particularly to the maintenance of U.S. interests in the first island chain that runs from Korea down through Japan and Taiwan and into South East Asia.

The Taiwan Relations Act clearly states that the U.S. will remain obligated *"to provide Taiwan with arms of a defensive character."* The U.S. is Taiwan's primary military partner, and retains a close material relationship with the island that covers not only arms sales, but also cooperation on intelligence, training, maintenance, and logistics.

Past U.S. policy, particularly under the Obama Administration, focused significant efforts on the expansion of training and exchanges intended to improve Taiwan's ability to maintain a viable self-defense of the island. This has been an important and commendable development in bilateral defense ties. While it goes mostly unseen, it does have a material impact on the island's defenses.

In instances where U.S. commitments to Taiwan's defense are discreetly carried out, there has been stability and ingenuity in expanding cooperation, but where the commitment is overt – such as with U.S. arms sales under the TRA – there has been significant regression particularly since 2011.

Renewing Assurances: Strengthening U.S.-Taiwan Ties

June 15, 2017

As of June 15, 2017 we have only seen a single sale of arms to Taiwan – in 2015 -since as far back as September 21, 2011. Since 2008, we have only seen one new platform capability being sold to Taiwan; the upgrade of Taiwan's legacy F-16 fleet to the F-16V format (bar a new engine).

While successive Republican and Democratic administrations have touted high dollar values for arms sales, a closer inspection of the trend lines show a material U.S. commitment in free fall. The Trump Administration has been handed a challenge to assess and deliver on a new range of commitments for Taiwan's national defense.

Taiwan currently has legitimate requirements for a number of systems, such as:
- New advanced fighters
- Electronic warfare aircraft
- New diesel-electric submarines
- Integrated command and control combat system for air defense
- An anti-ballistic missile defense system
- A remote sensing satellite system (SAR/EO)
- Medium-altitude, long-endurance unmanned aircraft system to gather intelligence as well as deploy air-to-surface missiles
- Modern towed and self-propelled artillery
- A Main Battle Tank

Additionally, the Trump Administration should also consider and implement:

- Mobile Training Teams on six month rotations at brigade level and above for English and advisory missions
- Formal agreement on a shared common operational platform (COP)
- Annual 2+2 meetings (senior DoD & State meeting with their Taiwan counterparts)
- A Joint Work Plan for future bilateral defense relations
- Expanded Taiwan military training in the U.S., to include the Taiwan Army and Navy

As Taiwan seeks to grow its domestic defense industry, it is also in a strong position to add value to America's industrial partnerships and to expand American defense exports. Therefore, the USTBC recommends that the Trump Administration invite Taiwan to participate at the Tier 2 level of several ongoing service programs. Taiwan turned down the opportunity to participate as a Tier 2 partner for the F-35 program, and lost an opportunity to secure access to the fighter at an early stage while simultaneously integrating Taiwan industry into the fighter's supply chain. Moving ahead on such participation in the future could be an important strategic action binding the two sides closer together.

Taiwan's defense spending is presently under 2% of its GDP. This remains unacceptable, and results in underfunding for Taiwan's military modernization goals and the goal of moving toward an all-volunteer force. As then Deputy Assistant Secretary of Defense Richard Lawless noted in 2005 at a USTBC conference, *"We cannot help defend you, if you cannot defend yourself."* These words still stand true today as Taiwan continues to underinvest in its own self-defense.

Arms Sales Packaging
In 2008, after an extended freeze in the notification process, the Bush Administration adopted a policy of packaging congressional notifications for arms sales into bundles that were notified together. That packaging process was adopted in an attempt to fulfil U.S. defense commitments to Taiwan in a way that would be less objectionable to China.

Renewing Assurances: Strengthening U.S.-Taiwan Ties

June 15, 2017

Regrettably, this practice has been maintained since then, to increasingly damaging effect. The bundling of Congressional notifications has placed downward pressure on the willingness of the U.S. to sell arms to Taiwan, while simultaneously complicating Taiwan's ongoing force modernization and budgetary process.

The USTBC recommends that the Trump Administration end the policy of packaging, and return to a regularized process whereby Taiwan would be treated like other security assistance partners all the way from the U.S. accepting Letters of Request (LoRs) for Pricing & Availability (P&A) data through to consulting with and notifying Congress of an intention to sell arms to Taiwan.

China will object to any sale of arms by the United States to Taiwan, irrespective of size, capability, or value. The U.S. leadership is charged with assessing Taiwan's requests for material support based only on the merits of the platform and on the extent to which the sale will support our nation's broader Asia Pacific goals. U.S.-China policy – beyond the growing threat posed by Chinese forces amassed across from Taiwan – should not be a consideration in this area.

The TRA states that *"the United States decision to establish diplomatic relations with the People's Republic of China rests upon the expectation that the future of Taiwan will be determined by peaceful means"* and that *"any effort to determine the future of Taiwan by other than peaceful means, including by boycotts or embargoes, a threat to the peace and security of the Western Pacific area and of grave concern to the United States."* China's ongoing force modernization directed at invading Taiwan, along with its coercive military posture, therefore undermine the very premise of the 1979 switch in recognition.

Conclusions & Policy Recommendations

U.S. strategic interests in the Asia Pacific remain inexorably intertwined with our support of Taiwan's economy and national security. However, this aspirational goal is being undermined by an orchestrated and coercive PRC policy to weaken U.S. support for the island, and to restrict Taiwan's self-determination.

If the United States continues to rhetorically say the right things but materially fails to act, then Taiwan risks being marginalized globally, and will be forced to interact with China from a weak position. The present trajectory could lead to a crisis in the Taiwan Strait – triggered by China's determination that the overall trilateral balance has tipped squarely in its favor and acting accordingly.

The US-Taiwan Business Council has a number of policy recommendations for the Trump Administration and the 115th U.S. Congress to consider. The USTBC recommends:

- That the U.S. launches negotiations with Taiwan for a Fair Trade Agreement (FTA) without preconditions
- That the Trump Administration undertakes an assessment of and commitment to the range of new defense capabilities presently being requested by Taiwan
- That the arms programs presently awaiting Congressional notification at the U.S. Department of State – including the 2007 notification for Taiwan's submarine program – be sent to Congress immediately
- That the Trump Administration ends the packaging of Congressional notifications for the sale of arms to Taiwan, returning to a regular, ongoing process
- That Taiwan should be encouraged to send significantly more Cabinet and sub-Cabinet level officials to the U.S. on a regular basis, to expand ties and to improve communication and cooperation
- That the Trump Administration undertakes sustained engagement by Cabinet officers in visiting Taiwan
- That U.S. policy is adjusted to allow for Assistant Secretaries from State and Defense to visit Taiwan.

Renewing Assurances: Strengthening U.S.-Taiwan Ties

June 15, 2017

Appendix

Table 1: Taiwan's Trade Ranking with the United States, 2004-2017

Year	Rank	Percentage of overall U.S. trade
2004	8	2.50%
2005	8	2.20%
2006	9	2.10%
2007	9	2.10%
2008	12	1.80%
2009	10	1.80%
2010	9	1.90%
2011	10	1.80%
2012	11	1.70%
2013	12	1.70%
2014	10	1.70%
2015	9	1.80%
2016	10	1.80%
2017 YTD	10	1.80%

Source: U.S. Census Bureau, *Top Trading Partners*

Table 2: Notified Taiwan Arms Sales Since 1990

Date	Notification	Est. Cost
Jul 1990	Cooperative Logistics Supply Support	0.108
Sep 1990	One C-130H transport aircraft	0.045
Jan 1991	100 MK-46 torpedoes	0.028
Jul 1991	97 SM-1 Standard air defense missiles	0.055
Sep 1991	110 M60A3 tanks	0.119
Nov 1991	Phase III PIP Mod Kits for HAWK air defense systems	0.17
May 1992	Weapons, ammunition, support for 3 leased ships	0.212
May 1992	Supply support arrangement	0.107
Aug 1992	207 SM-1 Standard air defense missiles	0.126
Sep 1992	150 F-16A-B fighters	5.8
Sep 1992	3 Patriot-derived Modified Air Defense System (MADS) fire units	1.3
Sep 1992	12 SH-2F LAMPS anti-submarine helicopters	0.161
Jun 1993	12 C-130H transport aircraft	0.62
Jun 1993	Supply support arrangement	0.156
Jul 1993	38 Harpoon anti-ship missiles	0.068
Jul 1993	Logistics support services for 40 leased T-38 trainers	0.07
Aug 1993	4 E-2T Hawkeye airborne early warning aircraft	0.7
Sep 1993	Logistics support services for MADS	0.175
Nov 1993	150 MK-46 Mod 5 torpedoes	0.054

Renewing Assurances: Strengthening U.S.-Taiwan Ties

June 15, 2017

Nov 1993	Weapons, ammunition, and support for 3 leased frigates	0.238
Nov 1993	MK-41 Mod Vertical Launch Systems for ship-based air defense missiles	0.103
Aug 1994	80 AN-ALQ-184 electronic counter measure ECM pods	0.15
Sep 1994	MK-45 Mod 2 gun system	0.021
Mar 1995	6 MK-75 shipboard gun systems, 6 Phalanx Close-In Weapon Systems	0.075
Jun 1995	Supply support arrangement	0.192
May 1996	Improved Mobile Subscriber Equipment communications system	0.188
May 1996	30 TH-67 training helicopters, 30 sets of AN-AVS-6 night vision goggles	0.053
May 1996	465 Stinger missiles, 55 dual-mounted Stinger launcher systems	0.084
Jun 1996	300 M60A3TTS tanks	0.223
Aug 1996	1,299 Stinger surface-to-air missiles, 74 Avenger vehicle mounted guided missile launchers, 96 HMMWVs (High-Mobility Multi-Purpose Wheeled Vehicle)	0.42
Sep 1996	110 MK-46 MOD 5 anti-submarine torpedoes	0.066
Feb 1997	54 Harpoon anti-ship missiles	0.095
May 1997	1,786 TOW 2A anti-armor guided missiles, 114 TOW launchers, 100 HMMWVs	0.081
Jul 1997	21 AH-1W Super Cobra helicopters	0.479
Sep 1997	13 OH-58D Kiowa Warrior Armed Scout helicopters	0.172
Nov 1997	Pilot training and logistics support for F-16 fighters	0.28
Nov 1997	Spare parts for various aircraft	0.14
Jan 1998	3 Knox-class frigates, 1 MK 15 Phalanx Close-In Weapons System	0.3
Jun 1998	28 Pathfinder-Sharpshooter navigation and targeting pods for F-16 fighters	0.16
Aug 1998	58 Harpoon anti-ship missiles	0.101
Aug 1998	61 Dual-mount Stinger surface-to-air missiles	0.18
Aug 1998	131 MK 46 Mod 5AS anti-submarine torpedoes	0.069
Oct 1998	9 CH-47SD Chinook helicopters	0.486
May 1999	240 AGM-114KS Hellfire II air-to-surface missiles	0.023
May 1999	5 AN-VRC-92E SINCGARS radio systems, 5 Intelligence Electronic Warfare systems, 5 HMMWVs	0.064
Jul 1999	Spare parts for F-5E-F, C-130H, F-16A-B, and IDF aircraft	0.15
Jul 1999	2 E-2T Hawkeye 2000E airborne early warning aircraft	0.4
Mar 2000	Modernization of the TPS-43F air defense radar to TPS-75V configuration	0.096
Mar 2000	162 HAWK Intercept guided air defense missiles	0.106
Jun 2000	39 Pathfinder-Sharpshooter navigation and targeting pods for F-16 fighters	0.234
Jun 2000	48 AN-ALQ-184 ECM pods for F-16s	0.122
Sep 2000	146 M109A5 howitzers, 152 SINCGARS radio systems	0.405
Sep 2000	200 AIM-120C AMRAAMs for F-16 fighters	0.15
Sep 2000	71 RGM-84L Harpoon anti-ship missiles	0.24
Sep 2000	Improved Mobile Subscriber Equipment IMSE communication system	0.513
Jul 2001	JTIDS Consoles and Related Equipment and Support	0.725
Sep 2001	AGM-65G Maverick Missiles and Related Equipment and Support	0.018
Oct 2001	Javelin Anti-Tank Missiles and Related Equipment and Support	0.051
Oct 2001	Cooperative Logistics Supply Support Arrangement	0.288
Jun 2002	Air Traffic Control Radar	0.108
Sep 2002	Rebuilt Standard Assault Amphibious Personnel Vehicles	0.25

Renewing Assurances: Strengthening U.S.-Taiwan Ties

June 15, 2017

Sep 2002	Maintenance of Repairable Material	0.174
Sep 2002	AIM-9M-1/2 Missiles	0.036
Sep 2002	AGM-114M3 HELLFIRE II Air-to-Surface Anti-Armor Missiles	0.06
Oct 2002	TOW-2B missiles	0.018
Nov 2002	KIDD Class Guided Missile Destroyers	0.875
Sep 2003	Multifunctional Information Distribution Systems/Low Volume Terminals	0.775
Mar 2004	Ultra High Frequency long range early warning radars	1.776
Oct 2005	Missiles and Pilot Training Program	0.28
Feb 2007	AMRAAM and Maverick missiles	0.421
Aug 2007	AGM-84L HARPOON Block II missiles	0.125
Sep 2007	SM-2 Block IIIA STANDARD missiles	0.272
Sep 2007	Excess P-3C aircraft	1.96
Nov 2007	PATRIOT Configuration 2 Ground Systems Upgrade	0.939
Oct 2008	30 AH-64D Block III APACHE Longbow Attack Helicopters	2.532
Oct 2008	32 UGM-84L Sub-Launched HARPOON Block II missiles and 2 UTM-84L HARPOON Block II Exercise missiles	0.2
Oct 2008	Upgrade of four E-2T Aircraft to the HAWKEYE 2000 configuration	0.25
Oct 2008	330 PATRIOT Advanced Capability (PAC-3) missiles	3.1
Oct 2008	Spare parts in support of F-5E/F, C-130H, F-16A/B, and Indigenous Defense Fighter IDF aircraft, communication equipment, radar, and other related elements of logistics support	0.334
Oct 2008	182 JAVELIN guided missile rounds and 20 JAVELIN command launch units	0.047
Jan 2010	UH-60M BLACK HAWK helicopters	3.1
Jan 2010	Multifunctional Information Distribution Systems/Low Volume Terminals (MIDS/LVT-1)	0.34
Jan 2010	OSPREY Class Mine Hunting Ships	0.105
Jan 2010	ATM-84L and RTM-84L HARPOON Block II Telemetry missiles	0.037
Jan 2010	PATRIOT Advanced Capability (PAC-3)Firing Units, Training Unit, and Missiles	2.81
Sep 2011	F-16 pilot training program	0.5
Sep 2011	Retrofitting of F-16A/B aircraft	5.3
Sep 2011	Spare parts in support of F-16A/B, F-5E/F, C-130H, and Indigenous Defense Fighter (IDF) aircraft	0.052
Dec 2015	208 Javelin Missiles	0.057
Dec 2015	Block I-92F MANPAD Stinger Missiles and Related Equipment and Support	0.217
Dec 2015	2 Oliver Hazard Perry Class Frigates	0.19
Dec 2015	MIDS/LVT-1 and JTIDS Follow-on Support	0.12
Dec 2015	Taiwan Advanced Tactical Data Link System (TATDLS) and Link-11 Integration	0.075
Dec 2015	36 Assault Amphibious Vehicles (AAVs)	0.375
Dec 2015	TOW 2B Aero RF Missiles, support and training	0.268
Dec 2015	MK 15 Phalanx Block 1B Baseline 2 Close-in Weapons System (CIWS) Guns, Upgrade Kits, Ammunition, and Support	0.416

Estimated Cost in US$ Billion

Sources: Defense Security Cooperation Agency (www.dsca.mil)

Kan, Shirley A. *"Taiwan: Major U.S. Arms Sales Since 1990"* CRS Report RL30957, June 13, 2014

Renewing Assurances: Strengthening U.S.-Taiwan Ties

June 15, 2017

Fact Check: The Media as a Useful Tool for Chinese Propaganda

- Chronic poor reporting on Taiwan by U.S. and international media is undermining the island. Western media unthinkingly parroting Chinese propaganda is an effective component of China's information warfare strategy.
- The referenced Panama statement actually echoes China's "*One-China Principle*." This is different and distinct from the U.S. "*One-China Policy*." The U.S. has never stated that Taiwan is a "breakaway province" – this is the Chinese position. Conflating the two is in China's interests, as part of its ongoing attempts to re-define all "*One-China*" interpretations to match its own version.
- The article presents only China's position on the Panama development, with no attempt to get the Taiwan government side of the story.
- The last arms sales package to Taiwan was in 2015, not 2016, and it ended a drought of over 4 years since the previous sale.

<u>**Excerpts from USA TODAY**</u>

What is the 'One China' policy?
June 13, 2017
https://www.usatoday.com/story/news/2017/06/13/what-is-one-china-policy/102806774/

Panama cut ties with Taiwan on Tuesday, switching its diplomatic relations to the People's Republic of China and **accepting the "One China" policy**. "The Government of the Republic of Panama recognizes that there is only one China in the world," the joint statement said. "The government of the People's Republic of China is the only legitimate government representing all China, and Taiwan is an inalienable part of the Chinese territory."
...

With Panama's departure from Taiwan's diplomatic cadre, that leaves just 20 or so nations with official, ambassador-level diplomatic ties to the island. **Most nations, including the United States, have accepted the "One China" policy.**

OK, so, what is the One China policy?
The U.S. recognition of **a "One China" policy** stems from 1979, when the U.S. switched diplomatic recognition from Taiwan to the People's Republic of China (PRC). In the 1979 U.S.-PRC Joint Communique, **the United States recognized the communist leadership in Beijing as the sole legal government of China, acknowledging the Chinese position that there is one China and Taiwan is a breakaway province that is part of China.**

"The Taiwan question bears on China's sovereignty and territorial integrity and touches our core interests," Chinese foreign ministry **spokesman Geng Shuang said in January after President Trump questioned the "one China" policy. "Adherence to the one China principle serves as the political foundation for the development of China-U.S. ties.** If this foundation is wobbled and weakened, then there is no possibility for the two countries to grow their relations in a sound and steady way and cooperate on key areas."
...

It hasn't always been easy ...
Earlier this year, China and the U.S. had a falling out when **Trump questioned the "One China" policy**. Trump broke with years of diplomatic protocol following his election when he accepted a congratulatory phone call from Taiwan President Tsai Ing-wen and again riled the Chinese when, in an interview with The Wall Street Journal in January, he said: "Everything is under negotiation, including **One China." From the Chinese perspective, that**

policy is non-negotiable.

...

<u>The U.S. seems to do a lot of business with Taiwan. What's up with that?</u>
Officially, the U.S. government does not support independence for Taiwan, a democracy that elects its own president and parliament. U.S. relations with the island are governed by the 1979 Taiwan Relations Act, which outlines the U.S. commitment to help Taiwan maintain its military defense. **Last year, the U.S. approved $1.8 billion in arms sales to Taipei.**

...

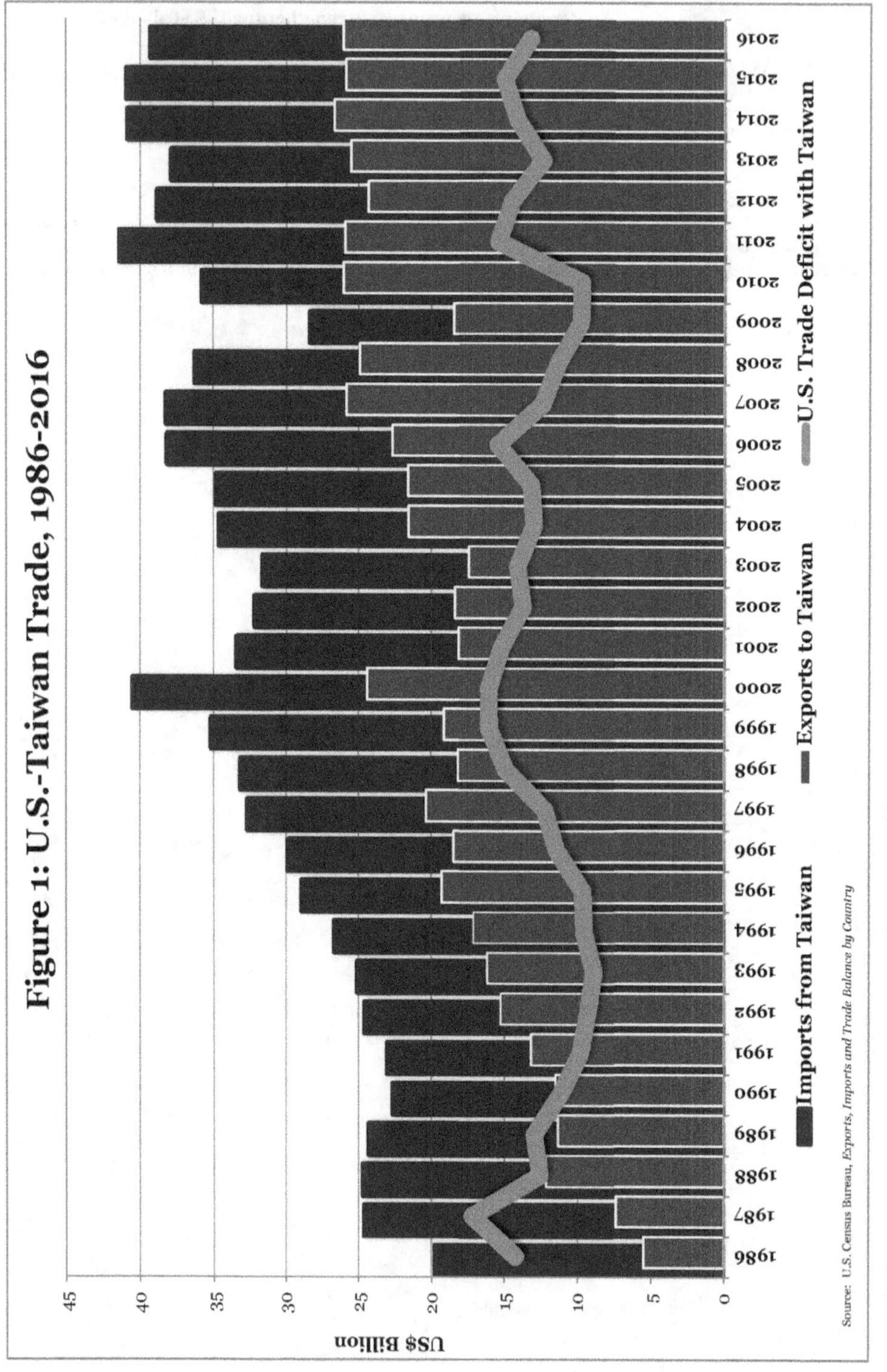

Figure 1: U.S.-Taiwan Trade, 1986-2016
US$ Billion
Imports from Taiwan
Exports to Taiwan
U.S. Trade Deficit with Taiwan
Source: U.S. Census Bureau, Exports, Imports and Trade Balance by Country

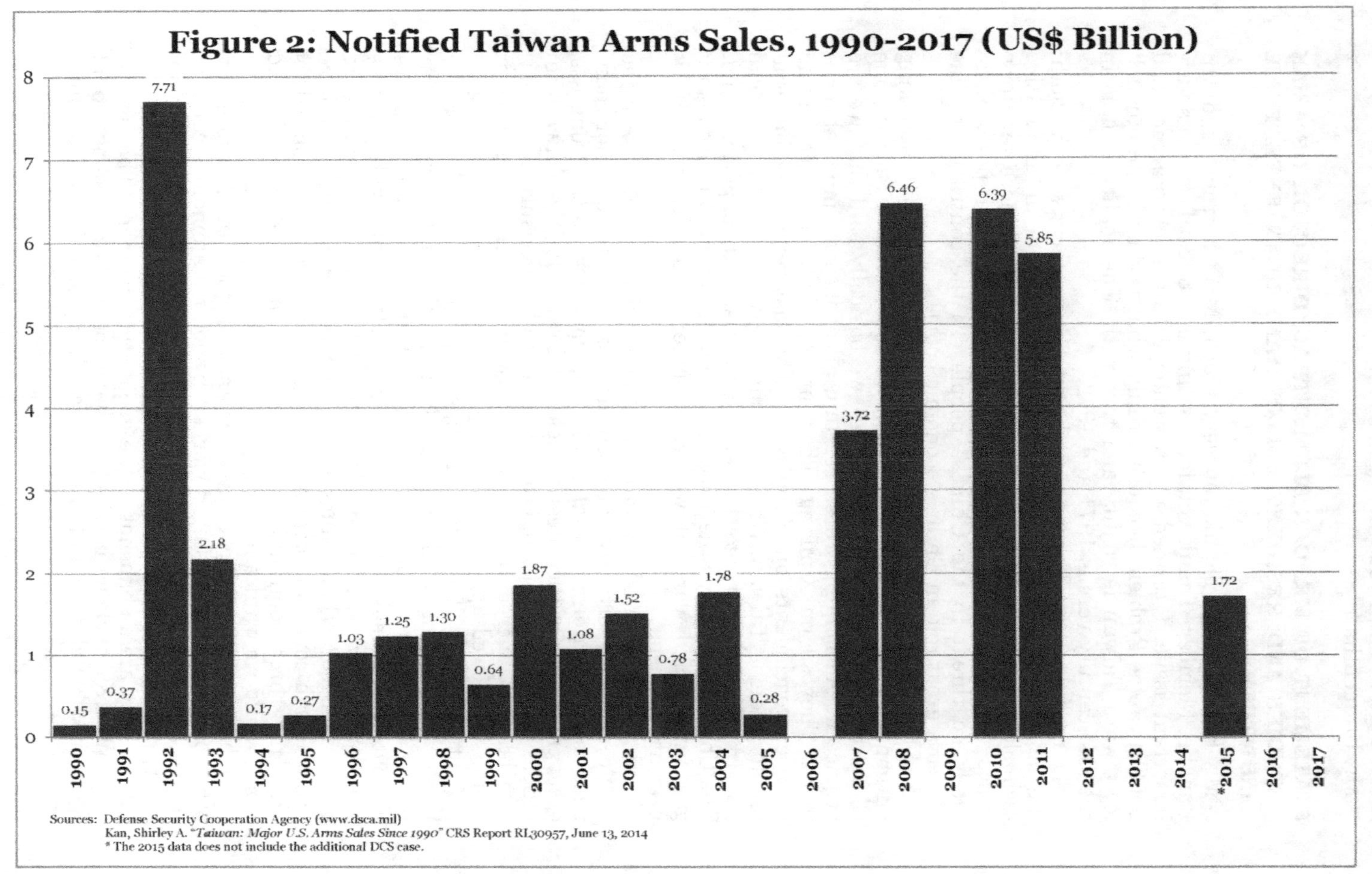

Figure 2: Notified Taiwan Arms Sales, 1990-2017 (US$ Billion)

Sources: Defense Security Cooperation Agency (www.dsca.mil)
Kan, Shirley A. *"Taiwan: Major U.S. Arms Sales Since 1990"* CRS Report RL30957, June 13, 2014
* The 2015 data does not include the additional DCS case.

Mr. YOHO. Thank you, Mr. Chambers.
Mr. Blumenthal?

STATEMENT OF MR. DAN BLUMENTHAL, DIRECTOR OF ASIAN STUDIES AND RESIDENT FELLOW, AMERICAN ENTERPRISE INSTITUTE

Mr. BLUMENTHAL. Thank you very much, Mr. Chairman and Mr. Ranking Member. Thank you for inviting me to testify on this very important issue. I termed my testimony, Taiwan as Partner and not Taiwan as Problem because I think what is missing in our policy toward Taiwan is reality and the truth. The reality is it is in the 21st century versus 1971 and 1972.

The reality is that Taiwan is a thriving democracy, wishing nothing more than to develop peacefully into more of an innovative technological powerhouse. It makes no claim on Chinese territory, it has abandoned the Chinese civil war long ago, and it poses absolutely no threat to the Chinese people. To the contrary, it has played a great role in China's economic boom.

And let's be very clear about what the PRC is doing. It is making an imperial claim on Taiwan. When we acquiesced in China's One China Policy—they call it Principle—we basically said that we are acquiescing in helping China reattain all of its lost imperial territories. They sit on Xinjiang. They sit on Tibet. They are having more encroachments on Hong Kong. The last remaining imperial territory left is Taiwan. Now there may have been good reason to do so back then, but let's be very clear this is an imperial claim. The Chinese may say otherwise. They may say there are issues regarding the civil war, but we are, in essence, acquiescing to Chinese imperialism.

This is surely an oddity in today's international relations. In the 21st century we certainly don't see the United States or other countries acquiescing on imperial ambitions. Obviously to the Congress' great credit, one of the finest things it did was pass the Taiwan Relations Act at the time and adhere to it and make sure the executive branch adhered to it so that Taiwan wouldn't become completely swallowed up.

A little history if you will indulge me. Back then China badly needed an opening with us. They had the Soviet Union on their border. They wanted to attack Vietnam. I am not so sure what we got out of that deal. That is for the historians. But I will ask this question. Are we still getting bad deals with China? Has anything really changed? When things float up in the foreign policy sphere about fourth communiques and so forth, we have to ask ourselves have the three communiques served our interests? Why in the world would we want a fourth?

We have to actually ask ourselves another question. Is there any other bilateral relationship governed by joint statements, communiques, and diplomatic snapshots of the moment rather than by treaty or anything else? What force do communiques have in diplomacy? They are a snapshot of the geopolitical moment. That is history. We are stuck with what we have today. We probably could have and should have gotten dual recognition of Taiwan and China in the 1970s like we did with Germany. Maybe we won't get it today, but there are still many options that we have to keep increasing Taiwan's autonomy and well-being.

Quickly, defense. We have all mentioned it. Taiwan could absolutely do more on its defense budget. But I was a Bush appointee during the $30 billion arms package to Taiwan. Taiwan has bought every single item on that package that we offered to them, besides the submarines, and that is because we have been playing games with the submarines. They will buy. Their defense budget will sky-rocket if we make things on offer.

But we should go further than just cross-Strait relations. Taiwan should be an integral part of our first island chain defense strategy. It is a harder target than the Philippines. If we sell the right things and engage in the right security cooperation with Taiwan it will make it harder for China to break out into the Pacific Ocean with impunity.

Let me skip trade, although it is very important. Let me just say this in closing. It is the height of fantasy to think that we can go forward with any building of Asian order without Taiwan. Taiwan is a claimant in the South China Sea. Taiwan is a more advanced economy than a lot of the TPP countries that entered. In fact, from an economic viewpoint it would be easy to do an FTA with Taiwan. The only thing holding us back is our reluctance with China.

We can't just sit here and ignore the fact that Taiwan sits in the middle, geostrategically, between Northeast and Southeast Asia. We can't have a South China Sea policy without Taiwan. And conversely, if Taiwan does fall into the hands of China, it will badly impinge upon our security interest with respect to the Japan alliance in the Pacific Ocean. So, Taiwan is, in reality, a partner, a key partner, and there is a lot more we can do to integrate it into the Asian order because the reality is it is already part of it. Thank you.

[The prepared statement of Mr. Blumenthal follows:]

Statement before the House Committee on Foreign Affairs
Subcommittee on Asia and the Pacific
On Renewing Assurances: Strengthening U.S.-Taiwan Ties

Taiwan as Partner, not Problem

Daniel Blumenthal
Director of Asian Studies

June 15, 2017

Mr. Chairman (Rep. Ted Yoho) Ranking member (Rep. Brad Sherman)

Thank you for inviting me to testify before you today alongside my two distinguished colleagues. Though China's aggressive activities in the South China Sea, rivalry with Japan, and the persistent crisis on the Korean Peninsula loom as large and dangerous matters, relations across the Strait are still arguably the biggest issue of contention between the US and the People's Republic of China (PRC).

Allow me to boil the problem down to its essence: Taiwan is a thriving democracy, wishing nothing more than to continue to peacefully develop into an innovative technology powerhouse. It makes no claims on Chinese territory and poses no threat to the Chinese people. To the contrary, Taiwan has played a major role in the China economic boom. However, the PRC makes an imperial claim to the island based on the fact that its last great empire conquered Taiwan hundreds of years ago. It gives Taiwan no quarter, as we just witnessed with Beijing's pressure on Panama to de-recognize Taiwan.

To be sure, there are other reasons why the People's Republic of China claims Taiwan – the legacy of the Chinese civil war and geostrategic considerations associated with China's attempted naval break-out into what we call the "first island chain."

But the bottom line is this: when we acknowledged in our first joint Communiqué with the PRC in 1972 "that all Chinese on either side of the Taiwan Strait maintain there is but one China and that Taiwan is part of China," we acquiesced in the Chinese project of putting back together its lost empire. With Xinjiang and Tibet firmly under the Chinese Communist Party's control, and Hong Kong losing its political autonomy, China is on its way to "re-unifying" its empire.

This is an oddity in contemporary international relations. Surely other countries are trying to re-establish their imperial borders – but China has already gained begrudging acceptance from much of the free world in its imperial ambitions, and Taiwan alone stands in the way.

To Congress' great credit, Taiwan was not swallowed up. Passage of the Taiwan Relations Act saved an ally from being destroyed.

China gained much back then– the breaking of our diplomatic ties and treaty with Taiwan, relief from Soviet pressure on their borders, and the freedom of action to attack Vietnam in 1979. What we gained is still open to academic debate. But here is a timely question: has this pattern of China getting the better end of deals with us really changed?

When new ideas, such as negotiating a 4th communiqué, are floated in high government circles, the first question should be: did the first three really benefit us? Are we better off without diplomatic recognition of Taiwan –without an arrangement where we recognize both Taiwan and China like we did with the two Germanys?   Deterrence is best served with clarity, and China may yet take advantage of our uneven commitment to Taiwan.

The Communiqués attempted to serve the geopolitical momentum, but that period is long-gone. Today, China is our most vexing strategic rival.

With this in mind, the geopolitical question of the moment should be: how can Taiwan advantage us in our rivalry with China? This is a much different way of framing our Taiwan relationship. Our default position is to think about how to manage the Taiwan "problem" so that it doesn't get in the way of our China relations.

I would humbly urge Congress to frame its legislative agenda in those terms – what more could we do with Taiwan that would help it thrive in ways that advantage our strategic competition with China?

We lost our chance at dual recognition because of a rushed and messy process of normalizing relations with China. However, we still have some options to help maintain Taiwan's autonomy and serve our interests:

1) **Defense** – While it is true that Taiwan does not always demonstrate an adequate urgency about the threats it faces, we don't always provide them with the opportunity to do so. The Taiwan defense budget would skyrocket if we put on offer the submarines, or the manned or unmanned aircrafts that Taiwan asks for.

    a. But we should go further. We need only consult a map to see that Taiwan can play an integral part in a strategy of defending the "first island chain," which would make it harder for China to break out into the Pacific Ocean with impunity.

2) **Trade** – The agenda of trade liberalization has seriously lost momentum. Finalizing trade agreements with advanced countries like Taiwan would rebuild new momentum. Taiwan would go far in opening its markets and ridding itself of tariffs. As the Trump Administration goes forward with bilateral FTAs, Taiwan could quickly become part of a free trade area of East Asia.

    a. Either we will set the rules and standards on tariffs, SOEs, IP, standards, and investment, or China will. Taiwan is a great place to begin (as is Japan).

3) **Integration into a still nascent Asian regional order** – It is the height of fantasy to think that a durable order favorable to our values and interests can form without Taiwan.

It is a claimant in the South China Sea dispute as well as a key player in global high-tech supply chains. And it is living proof, during a time of democratic black-sliding, that liberal democracy can take root in any society.

To conclude, with some ingenuity and creativity in Taipei and DC, Taiwan could be a partner in a robust US defense posture in the Asia-Pacific, in the creation of a "gold standard" free trade area in Asia, and in shaping a favorable regional order.

Thank you very much.

Mr. YOHO. Thank you, Mr. Blumenthal, for those informative statements, and I look forward to getting into the questions.

Mr. Hsiao?

STATEMENT OF MR. RUSSELL HSIAO, EXECUTIVE DIRECTOR, GLOBAL TAIWAN INSTITUTE

Mr. HSIAO. Thank you, Chairman Yoho and Ranking Member Sherman, for inviting me to testify before this subcommittee. This is truly an honor for me to be a part of this important and timely proceeding with my copanelists whom I deeply respect.

It has been over a year now since the subcommittee last held a hearing on Taiwan. A lot has happened since then. I would like to point out three clusters of developments for the subcommittee's considerations. First, President Tsai Ing-wen's historical election in January 2016 as the government's first female President sets a positive standard for other democracies worldwide.

In addition to electing a female head of government, Taiwan's Supreme Court recently issued a landmark ruling that invalidates a civil code provision prohibiting same-sex union. This act further raises Taiwan's profile in the league of progressive and liberal nations. According to the independent watchdog organization Freedom House, which monitors freedom and democracy worldwide, Taiwan ranked third most free in the Asia-Pacific, only behind Australia and Japan. While no democracy is perfect, democratization has had a moderating effect on Taiwan's fractious politics, which is clearly illustrated in the measured policies of the ruling government, and through the opposition Nationalist Party's chairperson election last month.

On cross-Strait, political relations between Taipei and Beijing has cooled as the PRC refuses to deal with the Tsai administration unless she accepts the so-called 1992 Consensus. While formal channels of communications between the PRC's Taiwan Affairs Office and to Taiwan's Mainland Affairs Council remains shut after Beijing froze dialogue back in June 2016, functional channels for coordination between different government agencies remain open. As a Chinese-speaking democracy, Taiwan has a unique role to play in China's future, but that role must not come at the expense of the freedom and democracy that the people of Taiwan have fought for and now enjoy.

The chilling case of the detained human rights activists, Lee Ming-che, who has been in detention since March 19th, throws into sharp relief the impact that China's non-democratic system has for Taiwan and its people, and also for Hong Kong. As the 2014 student-led protests in Taiwan and Hong Kong illustrate, what happens in Taiwan has a demonstration effect on Hong Kong, and what happens in Taiwan has a demonstration effect on Taiwan.

Despite Taipei's measured approach to cross-Strait relations, Beijing fired the first salvo that ignited cross-Strait tensions only 1 month after Tsai Ing-wen was elected President.

In February 2016, the PRC resumed diplomatic ties with Gambia. December 2016, Sao Tome and Principe switched diplomatic recognition. In January 2017, Nigeria announced that it was demoting ties with Taiwan by forcing Taipei to move its representative office from Abuja to Lagos. Panama's announcement just Tuesday that it had switched diplomatic recognition to PRC is the latest in a series of escalatory steps in Beijing's enhanced pressure tactics against Taiwan that include economic, military, and diplomatic coercion. It was only a matter of time before Beijing pulled the trigger.

Taiwan's informal ties with countries like the United States, India, Japan, Australia, and Singapore are now more important than ever as Beijing squeezes Taiwan's international and diplomatic space further. Specifically, more efforts need to be made to upgrade Taiwan's ability to engage the international community by including Taiwan in not only bilateral, but also multilateral exchanges to offset Beijing's coercive full-court press on Taiwan's international space.

As a strategic effort to rebalance its foreign relations and economy, the Tsai government has reinvigorated a longstanding policy to diversify its economic outreach which is currently heavily concentrated on China to the growing markets in the Indo-Pacific. Through an all-of-government approach, Taiwan is attempting to forge closer economic links as well as deepen the people-to-people ties with 18 countries in Southeast Asia, South Asia, and Australasia. The new plan is also the natural outgrowth of demographic trends on the island as more immigrants come to the country and with more children born of mixed marriages.

And just as the United States looked toward Asia in the former administration's pivot to rebalance strategy, Taiwan is also looking south to capitalize on the growing markets as well as strategic importance of the region.

Against the backdrop of a growing military imbalance in the Strait, Taiwan has currently embarked on ambitious measures to strengthen its indigenous defense capabilities and industries. Taipei just released a new military strategy through its QDR.

As a percentage of total government spending, Taiwan currently spends up to 15 percent on defense and, in March, Taiwan's minister of National Defense targeted for military expenditures to rise to the proverbial 3 percent of GDP. In this context, it is worth at least asking ourselves why in the absence of a mutual defense treaty does the U.S. demand that Taiwan spend an arbitrary 3 percent of its GDP on defense while expecting less of our other allies and partners.

Second, we now have a new President of the United States, an unorthodox President, who has not only shown that he will be not held back by unnecessary diplomatic norms, he has also demonstrated a willingness to question policy dogmas. As President-elect, Trump made an important gesture by taking a congratulatory phone call with the President of Taiwan. For a conversation that lasted no more than 10 minutes and mainly involved an exchange of niceties, the blowback was disproportional and underscores the fragility of the U.S.-Taiwan relationship.

The administration has identified North Korea's nuclear program as a primary threat in East Asia. In its efforts to apply maximum pressure on Pyongyang to denuclearize, President Trump is clearly attempting to re-enlist the support of the Beijing to use its leverage over North Korea to stop its provocations. Interestingly, experts have noted that while Beijing's leverage over Pyongyang is significant relative to the United States' and Japan's because the two have little to none, Beijing's actual leverage over Pyongyang is perhaps very little. The fact that North Korea has launched 16 missiles in ten tests so far in 2017 may be evidence of that lack of leverage. Therefore, any anticipation of what a tradeoff may bring in terms of actual results must be measured by a dose or realistic expectation in what China can and is willing to do.

While there is no evidence to indicate that the administration is considering such a move, I would simply note this as caution for the administration to avoid entertaining such a seductive idea that has no legs. With that I will yield. Thank you.

[The prepared statement of Mr. Hsiao follows:]

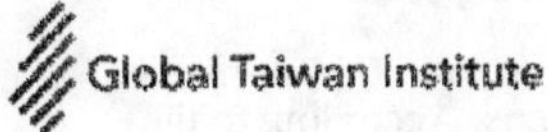

"Renewing Assurances: Strengthening U.S.-Taiwan Ties"

Testimony before

Subcommittee on Asia and the Pacific

House Committee on Foreign Affairs

United States House of Representatives

June 15, 2017

Russell Hsiao
Executive Director
Global Taiwan Institute

My name is Russell Hsiao. I am the Executive Director of the Global Taiwan Institute, a 501(c)(3) think tank dedicated exclusively to Taiwan policy research and public education. The views I express in this testimony are my own.

Thank you, Ranking Member Sherman and Chairman Yoho, for inviting me to testify before the subcommittee. This is truly an honor for me to be a part of this important and timely proceeding with my co-panelists whom I deeply respect.

It has been over a year now since this subcommittee last held a hearing on Taiwan and a lot has happened since then. Per your guidance, I would like to point out three clusters of developments for this subcommittee's considerations and provide explanations that illustrate their significance for the future of US-Taiwan relations. I hope these observations will help better inform the subcommittee as it deliberates how the United States might improve how we conduct relations with Taiwan under this new environment.

Taiwan

First, across the Pacific in Taiwan, President Tsai Ing-wen's historic election in the January 2016 election as the government's first female president sets a positive standard for other democracies worldwide. President Tsai has been in office now for over one year as her administration celebrated its one-year anniversary on May 20. I had the pleasure of being in Taiwan at that time and observed first-hand the people there after an eventful year of both ups and downs in US-Taiwan relations.

In addition to electing a female head of government, Taiwan's Supreme Court recently issued a landmark ruling that invalidates a civil code provision prohibiting same-sex union, which further raises Taiwan's profile in the league of progressive and liberal nations. According to the independent watchdog organization Freedom House, which monitors freedom and democracy worldwide, Taiwan ranked third most free in the Asia-Pacific, only behind Australia and Japan in its Freedom in the World 2017 report, and 40th among 211 entities studied in the report. While no democracy is perfect, democratization has had a moderating effect on Taiwan's fractious politics and clearly illustrated in the measured policies of the current ruling government and the Nationalist Party chairperson election last month.

Cross-Strait Relations

Political

On cross-Strait relations, political relations between Taipei and Beijing has cooled since the PRC refuses to deal with the Tsai administration unless she accepts the so-called "1992 consensus," a tacit agreement reached between the two sides 25 years ago in 1992 that agreed that the two sides belonged to One-China and agreed to differ as to their interpretation of its meaning. While formal channels between the People's Republic of China's (PRC) Taiwan Affairs Office and Taiwan's Mainland Affairs Council remain shut after Beijing froze government-to-government dialogue back in June 2016, functional channels for cooperation between different ministries remain open.

As a Chinese-speaking democracy, Taiwan has a unique role to play in China's future. But that role must not come at the expense of the freedom that the people of Taiwan have fought for and now enjoy. The chilling case of the detained human rights activists, Lee Ming-che—who has been in detention since March 19—throws into the sharp relief the impact that China's non-democratic system has for Taiwan and its people—and also for Hong Kong. The 20th anniversary of Hong Kong's retrocession to China will take place on July 1.

While the connection between Taiwan and Hong Kong goes back much farther, a sense of solidarity developed in 2014 after the youth-led protests in Taiwan and Hong Kong. The people of Taiwan are now keenly aware of the suppression of rights and freedoms that the people of Hong Kong face under PRC rule. That bond will likely only grow with time. Indeed, what happens in Hong Kong has a demonstration effect in Taiwan, and what happens in Taiwan has a demonstration effect in Hong Kong.

Military

As the Department of Defense's 2017 *China Military Power Report* indicates, Taiwan remains the People's Liberation Army's (PLA) main "strategic direction,"[1] which refers to one of the geographic areas the Chinese leadership identifies as endowed with strategic importance. Indeed, the Taiwan contingency is the primary driver of PLA defense planning. Towards that end, the PLA is developing anti-access/area denial capabilities to keep adversary forces that might deploy or operate within the western Pacific Ocean in the air, maritime, space, electromagnetic, and

---

[1] https://www.defense.gov/Portals/1/Documents/pubs/2017_China_Military_Power_Report.PDF

information domains farther at bay. The PLA reportedly has more than 1,500 missiles targeting Taiwan.

Against the backdrop of a growing military imbalance in the Strait, Taiwan is currently embarking on ambitious measures to strengthen its indigenous defense industries and capabilities. The Tsai administration just released a new military strategy through its Quadrennial Defense Review and reformulated its defense strategy to "resolute defense, multi-domain deterrence." As a percentage of total government spending, Taiwan currently spends up to 15% on defense,[2] and in March, Taiwan's Minister of National Defense targeted for military expenditures to rise to the proverbial 3% of gross domestic product in 2018.[3] In this context, it is worth at least asking ourselves why the US demands that Taiwan spend an arbitrary 3% of its GDP on defense while expecting less of her other allies and security partners?

Foreign Relations & Diplomatic Space

Despite Taipei's measured approach to cross-Strait relations, which is based on three pillars: 1) the ROC Constitution, 2) Act Governing Relations between the People of the Taiwan Area and the Mainland Area; and 3) the spirit of the 1992 meeting and subsequent negotiations, Beijing began unilaterally peeling off Taiwan's diplomatic allies and force other nations to degrade its unofficial relations with Taiwan.

Indeed, Beijing fired the first salvo that ignited the resumption of cross-Strait tension only one month after Tsai Ing-wen was elected president. In February 2016, the PRC decided to resume diplomatic ties with Gambia, which had broke diplomatic relations with Taiwan back in 2013; in December 2016, the small African nation of São Tomé and Principe switched diplomatic recognition over to the PRC, and in January 2017, Nigeria announced that it was demoting ties with Taiwan by forcing Taipei to move its representative office from Abuja to Lagos. There are signs that Beijing is enticing other countries to follow suit and indications are that other countries may be on the fence.

Panama's announcement on June 12 that it has switched diplomatic relations to the People's Republic of China is the latest in a series of escalatory steps in Beijing's enhanced pressure tactics against Taiwan that include economic, military, and also diplomatic coercion.

Panama had reportedly sought to establish diplomatic relations with the PRC since as early as 2008 but was told by PRC diplomats to "remain calm." It was only a matter of time before Beijing pulled the trigger despite the Tsai administration's pledge to maintain the "status quo" in cross-Strait relations. Considering the public support for the Tsai government's cross-Strait approach, rather than delegitimize the government in the eyes of its people—which is Beijing's probable intent—its actions will likely be counter-productive and fuel greater public angst and animosity towards the PRC.

---

[2] http://www.taipeitimes.com/News/taiwan/archives/2017/03/05/2003666171
[3] https://www.bloomberg.com/politics/articles/2017-03-16/taiwan-plans-military-spending-increase-to-counter-rising-china

Taiwan's informal ties with countries like the United States, Japan, and India are now more important than ever as Beijing squeezes Taiwan's international and diplomatic space further. Specifically, more efforts need to be made to upgrade Taiwan's ability to engage the international community by including Taiwan in bilateral and multilateral exchanges to offset Beijing's coercive full-court press on Taiwan's international space.

While Beijing's pressure tactics weighs heavily on Taiwan's international space, there are significant improvements in Taiwan's unofficial relations with key economic and security partners besides the United States throughout the region that militate against these blows. Two stands out in particular: Japan and India.

Most notably, in January 2017, Tokyo changed the name of its *de facto* embassy in Taiwan from the Interchange Association, Japan to the Japan-Taiwan Exchange Association. In March 2017, the Senior Vice Minister of Internal Affairs and Communications visited Taiwan—the most senior government official to visit the island since the two sides severed diplomatic ties in 1972. Building off the positive momentum of the previous Ma administration's East China Peace Initiative, Taiwan and Japan have held multiple maritime dialogues. With New Delhi, the India-Taiwan Parliamentary Friendship Forum was formed by members of the lower house of India's bicameral parliament in December 2016 to facilitate high-level parliamentary exchanges between India and Taiwan.

Taiwan's New Southbound Policy

The Tsai government has also reinvigorated a long-standing policy to diversify its economic outreach, which is currently heavily concentrated in China, to the growing markets in the Indo-Pacific. Through an all-of-government approach, Taiwan is attempting to forge closer economic links as well as deepen people-to-people ties with 18 countries in Southeast Asia, South Asia and Australasia. The new plan is the natural outgrowth of demographic trends on the island, as more children are born of mixed marriages, and just as the United States looked towards Asia in the former administration's pivot/rebalance strategy, Taiwan is also looking south to capitalize on the growing markets and strategic importance of the region.

While the new plan is still in its infancy, the preliminary assessment appears to be fairly successful as Taiwan has been able to off-set the 18% drop in tourists from China with more tourists from Southeast Asia.[4] Moreover, the growing markets in the region have been receptive to the prospect of additional investments and trade with Taiwan, and the Taiwan government are creating the safety net mechanism to encourage the backbone of its economy, its small and medium enterprises, to take the necessary risks of doing business in the region.

Beijing's Squeeze on International Space

Beijing, however, appears intent on cranking the screw on Taiwan's international space. One opportunity after the other, Beijing authorities have leveraged its effective veto power of telling member countries to block Taiwan's participation in international bodies, even where diplomatic recognition was not a prerequisite. Taiwan was excluded from the International Civil Aviation

---

[4] http://www.dw.com/en/taiwan-reduces-reliance-on-mainland-chinese-tourists/a-37645694

Organization (ICAO) Conference in September 2016, the International Criminal Police Organization's (Interpol) 85th general assembly in November 2016, and most recently and perhaps egregious violation of decency and respect for human life, Taiwan was not permitted to participate in the World Health Assembly that was held last month. Also, in early May, Taiwanese participants to the intergovernmental dialogue on conflict diamond, Kimberly Process, hosted by Australia was ejected after the Chinese delegates interrupted the proceeding to protest Taiwan observing the dialogue.

United States

Second, we have a new president in the United States. An unorthodox president who has not only shown that he will not be held back by diplomatic conventions, he has also demonstrated a willingness to question policy dogmas, and expressed a penchant for unpredictability.

As president-elect, Trump made an important gesture by taking a congratulatory phone call from President Tsai Ing-wen in December 2016. This is the first time that the leaders of the United States and Taiwan spoke by phone, at least since 1979. For a conversation that lasted no more than 10 minutes and mainly involved an exchange of niceties, the blowback was disproportional and underscores the fragility, as well as complexity, of the US-Taiwan-China relationship.

US "One-China" policy

Flirting with suggestions of a shift in longstanding US 'policy,' Trump stated that "I fully understand the 'one China' policy, but I don't know why we have to be *bound* by a 'one China' policy unless we make a deal with China having to do with other things, including trade." The president-elect was correct. The US "One-China" policy is not law and thus has no binding effect on the executive branch. However, the perception that Trump would be willing to engage in what was perceivably a high-risk gamble gave rise to concerns that even Taiwan's interests may be traded away and used as a so-called "bargaining chip." Yet, on the other hand, the Taiwan Relations Act (TRA) is domestic law and has a binding effect. As the National Security Council senior director for Asia recently noted at a DC conference: "We are very much bound by the Taiwan Relations Act--*bound* to continue supporting Taiwan under that act."[5]

Regional Uncertainty

As the Chairman noted, all of this is occurring against a backdrop of growing regional uncertainty about the current administration's policies, strategy, and priorities.

The administration has identified North Korea's nuclear program as the primary threat in East Asia. In its effort to apply "maximum pressure" on Pyongyang to denuclearize, President Trump is clearly attempting to re-enlist the support of Beijing to use its leverage over North Korea to stop its provocations. Interestingly, experts have noted that while Beijing's leverage over Pyongyang is significant only relative to the United States' and Japan's because the two have little to none. Beijing's actual leverage over Pyongyang is, however, perhaps very little. The fact

---

[5] https://spfusa.org/event/fourth-annual-security-forum-u-s-japan-alliance-foundation-asian-security/

that North Korea has launched 16 missiles in 10 tests so far in 2017 may be evidence of that lack of leverage.

Therefore, any anticipation of what a tradeoff may bring in terms of actual results must be measured by a dose of realistic expectation in what China *can* and *is* willing to do. While there are no evidence to indicate that the administration is considering such a move, I would simply note as caution for the administration to avoid entertaining this seductive idea that has no legs.

Defense Secretary James Mattis' statement at the Shangri-La Dialogue reaffirming US defense commitments to Taiwan based on the TRA was a step in the right direction. More can and should be done.

China

Third, Beijing is not only not reciprocating Tsai's overtures, it has ratcheted up pressure against Taipei. Rather than talk to Tsai, Xi has focused on courting a weakened opposition, applying economic pressure on Taiwan to stir domestic discontent, and squeezing Taiwan's international space in a full court press to coerce Taipei into submitting to the PRC. The effect has been counterproductive to Beijing's stated aim to resolve the issue peacefully. While its objective remains the same, there have been some interesting developments related to Beijing's approach to Taiwan.

New Approach, Same Strategy, Old Policy

Most notably, there have been a number of interesting appointments in the PRC's Taiwan policy apparatuses over the last year that appears to signal a change in how Beijing may *approach* the Taiwan issue. Two appointments stand out.

At the PRC's premier research institution the Chinese Academy of Social Sciences, the Institute of Taiwan Studies' new director Yang Minjie was the former Vice President of CICIR, a Ministry of State Security-affiliated research institution. Yang's expertise is in regional security and notably not a Taiwan-expert. This is a clear departure from his predecessor who was steeped on Taiwan affairs work. The second interesting appointment is that of senior statesmen Dai Bingguo as head of the National Society of Taiwan Studies. A national body, which has more than 40 member organizations, 1,000 individual members, 40 executive council members, and 180 councilors including senior representatives from state-run media, central government offices, various government agencies under the State Council, the Academy of Military Science, and government research centers.

I must stress, however, that these appointments should not be seen to indicate that the PRC has changed its longstanding policy on Taiwan. Policy remains set at the CCP's Leading Taiwan Affairs Leading Small Group headed by Xi Jinping. The all powerful Standing Committee of the CCP Politburo is set to change at the upcoming 19th Party Congress.

19th Party Congress

The CCP is in the process of an important leadership transition that will take place this Fall. The transition will see a wholesale change in the make-up of the Standing Committee of CCP

Politburo and the political sensitivity surrounding the situation is palpable. One plausible explanation for Xi's apparent heavy-handed tactics is perhaps due to a need to appear strong in the face of power jockeying that is inevitably occurring behind closed doors in Zhongnanhai.

East China Sea and South China Sea Linked to Taiwan

Over the past decade, Beijing has been increasingly aggressive over territorial disputes in the East China Sea and South China Sea. In addition to increased military exercises and confrontations with navies and coast guards in the region, Beijing established an Air Defense Identification Zone in the East China Sea in 2013 and there are reasons to think that it may do so for the South China Sea as well. As USPACOM Commander Admiral Harry Harris stated, Beijing is building a "Great Wall of Sand" in the South China Sea. I agree with the Chairman's assessment that these efforts appear to be directed at "boxing Taiwan in."[6] Indeed, Taiwan remains the primary driver of Chinese defense investments and planning, therefore a Taiwan contingency must remain the focus of United States defense planners.

Economic Coercion

Beijing does not hide the fact that it views its economic relationship with Taiwan and other countries as leverage. One recent manifestation of this coercive strategy is Beijing's control of tourists from the PRC going to Taiwan to apply pressure on Taiwan's economy.

Despite the drop in tourists from China, total number of tourists to Taiwan actually increased 2.4% in 2016. This growth was driven by tourists coming from other Asian countries such as Thailand, Vietnam, the Philippines, Malaysia, Indonesia, Japan, and South Korea.

As noted earlier, Taiwan is not the only target of Beijing's economic coercion. In 2010, Beijing cut off exports of rare-earth minerals to Japan because of disputes over the Senkakus/Diaoyutai Islands. In 2012, Beijing barred the import of bananas from the Philippine after the Scarborough Shoal incident. In 2017, Beijing is applying pressure on South Korea over its deployment of THAAD.

In the face of Beijing's strategy of utilizing all levers of power, the United States should consider all means, as the TRA stipulates, "to maintain the capacity of the United States to resist any resort to force or other forms of coercion that would jeopardize the security, or the social or economic system, of the people on Taiwan."

Conclusion

On balance, President Trump's phone call with Tsai signaled nothing more than that his administration will not be bound unnecessarily to self-restrictive conventions that demean our relationship with a key security partner and democratic ally.

Despite the mainstream view that the Trump administration was going to break from longstanding US policy, his administration ultimately pursued an approach in US-Taiwan relations that hewed closely to a "status quo" that has persisted since 1979—in which two

---

[6] http://www.washingtonexaminer.com/lawmakers-china-gaining-influence-over-us-allies/article/2625597

legitimate governments co-exists across the Taiwan Strait, based on the Taiwan Relations Act, Six Assurances, and the US "One-China" policy.

While many things have happened, very little has changed.

Although the Strait is currently calmer now after President Trump reaffirmed the status quo by reaffirming the US "One-China" policy in his February phone call with Xi Jinping, it behooves this committee to be aware that while sustaining the status quo may be a viable short-to-medium term proposition, the status quo is not sustainable in the long-term.

The PLA's unprecedented military buildup, growing economic leverage, diplomatic coercion, and regional uncertainty over US staying power in the region, leaves Taiwan more susceptible to PRC coercion, and thus presents a risk to the peace and stability in the Western Pacific.

While allies and partners could and should do more for their own defense, the urgency of the challenges ahead demands cooperation, and the collective action of our allies and friends in the region. In this context, it is necessary to restore a consistent, high-level, and reliable process in how the United States engages with Taiwan on arms sales that will have the effect of reassuring our friends on Taiwan of US commitment to not only Taiwan but to regional allies and partners.

Alternatives to a gradual change in policy present equally destabilizing propositions. Yet a fear of even thinking about change could lead to state of paralysis that is equally disruptive in the Taiwan Strait. A one-sided focus on the process has left US interests increasingly susceptible to the vagaries of cross-Strait relations and Beijing's increasing leverages to coerce its desired political outcome.

Set against the region's geostrategic uncertainty and increasing pressure on the alliances, the United States needs an integrated approach that leverages diplomatic, military, and economic tools to strengthen relations with Taiwan and maintain its capacity to help Taiwan resist PRC coercion. This integrated approach requires a mix of hard and soft power to strengthen alliances and partnership, reduce uncertainty, and minimize miscalculation by all sides. A clearly stated objective of soft balancing to shore up the sovereignty gap in the Taiwan Strait would ensure lasting peace in the Taiwan Strait. Lastly, strategic accommodation of China, especially over Taiwan, would be a strategic mistake. Outsized expectation of China's leverage to rein in North Korea could disproportionately lead to a miscalculation of tradeoffs that would seriously damage US credibility with little gains.

Recommendations

The confluence of these factors brings me to my overall recommendation on the urgency for a gradual recalibration of US policy towards Taiwan.

First, especially in the aftermath of the break in diplomatic ties between Taiwan and Panama, I wish to commend Ranking Member Sherman and other distinguished members of this committee for passing the Taiwan Travel Act, which, as the committee rightfully finds, the United States should lift the self-imposed restrictions of high-level visits between officials at all levels of the United States Government, including cabinet-level national security officials, to and from

Taiwan. The current approach of conditioning the execution of US law and policy on Beijing's reaction in effects leads to creeping deference to Beijing's "One-China" principle, and the PRC should not be allowed to dictate how the United States conducts its informal relations with Taiwan.

Second, the Global Cooperation and Training Framework (GCTF), launched in 2015, is a critical mechanism for enhancing Taiwan's international space. It should be expanded and adequately resourced. Functional cooperation with Taiwan in "training programs for experts from throughout the region to assist them with building their own capacities to tackle issues where Taiwan has proven expertise and advantages" are a-political and Taiwan's meaningful participation in the international community must not be allowed to be curtailed by the PRC's calculated politicization of Taiwan's international space.

Third, the PRC massive military buildup across the Strait and its continued refusal to renounce the use of force against Taiwan is a threat to the peace and security of the Western Pacific area. While the United States has managed to deter Beijing from taking destructive military action against Taiwan over the last four decades because the latter has been relatively weak, the risks of this approach inches dangerously close to outweighing its benefits. Greater clarity of U.S. commitments to defend Taiwan is critical for purposes of deterrence and stability. As the PLA grows stronger, a perceived lack of commitment by the United States to defend Taiwan may further embolden Beijing to use force to resolve the Taiwan issue.

Fourth, in the face of Secretary of State Tillerson's comments downplaying basing foreign policy decisions on American values, Congress could reassert the importance of shared values in American foreign policy since "the foundation of US-Taiwan relations is our shared values—our commitment to democracy, civil liberties, and human rights."[7] It is at least reassuring to note that at his confirmation hearing, the Secretary Tillerson, stated that, "The people of Taiwan are friends of the United States and should not be treated as a bargaining chip. The US commitment to Taiwan is both a legal commitment and a moral imperative."[8]

Fifth, and perhaps most importantly, President Ronald Reagan's Six Assurances are necessary but no longer sufficient. Renewed assurances for Taiwan are needed in this period of growing uncertainty. Much has changed since the Six Assurances and other non-papers were issued back in 1982. In conjunction with the original assurances, renewed assurances could, as former Deputy Assistant Secretary of State for East Asian and Pacific Affairs Randy Schriver wrote, make clear that preserving Taiwan's democracy as an interest of the United States; honor the TRA; not pressure Taiwan into negotiations with the PRC; not support an outcome that does not enjoy the support among the majority of the free people of Taiwan; and not "co-manage" the Taiwan issue with the PRC.[9]

Ranking Member and Mr. Chairman, thank you again for this opportunity.

---

[7] http://docs.house.gov/meetings/FA/FA00/20140314/101903/HHRG-113-FA00-Wstate-MoyK-20140314.pdf
[8] http://focustaiwan.tw/news/aipl/201703080019.aspx
[9] http://www.taipeitimes.com/News/editorials/archives/2007/08/22/2003375330/2

Mr. YOHO. Thank you, gentlemen. I appreciate everybody's statement and your expertise. And that is what I rely on is your expertise to help draft policies of where we go. You know, we know where we come from. We have seen the changes happening in the Asia-Pacific Theater.

I was at a conference, I think it was a year ago when we were with a bunch of the generals, and they say we are going through a tectonic shift in world powers that we have not seen since World War II. Then if you parallel that or take that into consideration with what is going on in the Asia-Pacific Theater, the South China Sea, you see China making international claims to areas that they have never done this before. Historically, it has not been done. They are following the nine-dash lines and they start claiming sovereignty to areas and start building the islands in those areas, militarizing those islands.

We were at a hearing probably a year and a half ago with the Chinese Ambassador and he assured us that the Spratly Islands and the islands they were building were for peaceful navigational purposes. We just wrote an editorial about that giving our opinion on that and that is what it is, an opinion. But I think we can tell by the actions what China is doing with the intention of where they are going.

I read Robert Gates' book called Duty, and they were talking about the Taiwanese sales, and it was the last one that we had, and they were talking about how we have done this since 1979. China has kind of resisted a little bit, but that last one they resisted strongly. Our negotiator asked their admiral what was the big concern, we have done this 1979, and their response was this, and I think this is very poignant and very succinct on where their intentions are. The Chinese Ambassador said, I know you have, but we were weak then, we are strong now.

From that point forward you look at what they have been doing since then. They have been isolating Taiwan further and further. We saw what they did with the WHO. Taiwan researchers were so critical in the SARS epidemic with the research that they did that they should be invited regardless of who they are. I would want them at the table in those negotiations in those discussions, yet China says no, we want them out of here. We have seen them do that over and over again as you brought up what they have done in Africa, and those countries in Africa have pivoted from them.

We just saw what Panama—so I think the writing is on the wall with the direction. With them, them being China, building in the South China Sea and the world stood idly by and allowed them to become aggressive, if that aggression is not blocked, if that aggression—I don't want to say even blocked. If it is not challenged and said no, you can't do this, it is going to continue is what I see happening. I want to just read something here. A real pain you guys getting my reading.

A strong and economically prosperous Taiwan is in the interest of the United States and should be one of our core pillars of America's support for the island. I think that is very succinct and very direct on where we should stand and we should work harder to work with—I don't want to say the sovereignty of Taiwan, but recognizing Taiwan as who they are and not cross the bridge or cause trouble with the One China Policy because they have to deal with it. They are right there 110 miles off that coast.

So my question to you is how do we move forward to protect the independent nature of that relationship so that Taiwan can continue to flourish with the development, the economic prosperity, as Ranking Member Sherman said with the Freedom House index it was 1.5, now they are 1. I mean they are top of the scale—so that we don't go backwards? I know China feels threatened by that.

How do we bring that assurance so that we can continue the relationship that we have and build upon that? I would hope China would look at them as a great example of what can happen without fear.

Mr. Hammond-Chambers?

Mr. HAMMOND-CHAMBERS. Thank you, sir. Well, a couple of thoughts for sure. I would certainly state right off the bat that in my view the Taiwan Relations Act has the scope to handle the challenge that you have just posed. And that was really the genius, the vision of the TRA back in 1979, so I don't believe that there is a requirement to amend what was conceived back then.

But what we certainly need is more consistency particularly out of the executive branch on Taiwan policy. That certainly has undermined efforts particularly over the last 11 to 12 years, successive administrations, the absence of consistency and the growing pressure of course the Chinese have placed. It would help at a practical level if there was more consideration of Taiwan related initiatives separate of consideration of China.

What might illustrate that point is to point out to the committee that when you have representatives of the administration come up and speak to you, you will note that often the person responsible is responsible for both China and Taiwan. In my view that immediately puts Taiwan and the interests of the United States, vis-a-vis Taiwan, on a back foot, because that person will reflexively consider China when they consider Taiwan and that is always a larger account than it is on Taiwan front. So perhaps separating those, making a case to the executive branch that Taiwan should have more operating room within the interagency process and within different departments.

Mr. YOHO. I appreciate that and we are out of time. So I would love to hear from you two, but maybe if you can submit that, your thoughts on that to the record. Now we will go to Ms. Titus from Nevada, for 5 minutes.

Ms. TITUS. Thank you, Mr. Chairman, and thank you for holding this hearing. I am proud to consider myself a good friend of Taiwan. I represent a number of Taiwanese Americans in my district in southern Nevada, and I have had the privilege of visiting Taiwan to see the culture and the history and enjoy the food and all up close, so I thank you for your hospitality.

Throughout my time here in Congress too I have worked to strengthen the relationship between Taiwan and the United States supporting military sales to Taiwan, and Taiwan's efforts to join international organizations. Something that is especially relevant to my district is expanding the visa waiver program so people from Taiwan can visit without having to have a visa. Last year, we welcomed close to ½ million Taiwanese visitors and that included about 50,000 to Las Vegas.

As a representative of Las Vegas, and we love visitors. That is something I would like to ask you about. If you haven't been to Las Vegas, please come and see us. I just would ask any members of the panel, first, what do you think that we might be able to do specifically in promoting tourism, more tourism between the United States and Taiwan as we look to strengthen our relations both politically and economically?

Mr. HAMMOND-CHAMBERS. On the tourism front, as you correctly pointed out, there is already a significant Taiwan population here. I think some advertising in Taiwan certainly would help. I think if the U.S. is looking to raise the number of Taiwanese visiting the United States, advertising specific places like Las Vegas, the incoming NFL team that you have. The Taiwan citizens are voracious followers of American professional sports teams and Vegas appears to be on a roll in that regard.

Ms. TITUS. So to speak that is right.

Mr. HAMMOND-CHAMBERS. I think you have hockey and football arriving imminently and surely basketball and baseball will follow in time, which is a very exciting time for you. Taiwan citizens follow American sports and that might be something worth advertising to them.

Ms. TITUS. It is interesting. We have a program, Brand USA, where we have tried advertising in parts of Europe. Maybe we need to look at not at cutting that program, which has been very successful, but expanding it.

Mr. Blumenthal or anybody else?

Mr. BLUMENTHAL. On tourism I think that first of all, going the other direction, a number of newspapers and magazines have now claimed or reported that Taiwan is one of the best tourist destinations for Americans and the top place for expats to live when they do business. In terms of Taiwanese coming here, I think Rupert Hammond-Chambers has some good ideas. I think casinos and Las Vegas are something the people of Taiwan enjoy and perhaps share that enjoyment if we are looking at people to people talks between the Chinese and Taiwanese, they share that enjoyment with their mainland friends. I think they are going to build some big casinos in Taiwan. I think they are a big attraction as well, so I think it will always be a place the Taiwanese want to go.

Mr. HSIAO. Thank you for that question and let me just echo my colleagues' comments so far. I would also just add that the United States remains one of the favorite destinations for Taiwanese people to travel to, I think, and the soft power of the United States in terms of its appeal to the people of Taiwan, students, is, I think, not matched by any other country in the world.

So improving on that I think is, while I think it is certainly a worthwhile and important goal to strive towards, I think there is already a high standard there that we are working on and I think to improve that I think is to deepen that relationship in a way so that we cultivate emerging leaders who are going to be future leaders of both the United States and Taiwan, so that connection is on an even deeper level. I think programs that would be able to encourage that would be a vehicle to work towards. Thank you.

Ms. TITUS. Maybe even some exchanges with UNLV's School of Hospitality or that sort of thing. Just real quickly, Mr. Chairman, I want to go back to a point that you just made, Mr. Hammond-Chambers. I too share your concern about the mixed messages coming out of this administration, not just to Taiwan but to the whole rest of the world. We don't seem to know who is in charge. Is it the President, is it the Secretary of State, is it the non-appointed undersecretary? So I think we should really pay attention to the need to get our foreign policy in order and not just made from Twitter to Twitter.

Mr. YOHO. The chair will now recognize Mr. Chabot who used to be the chairman of the Asia-Pacific Subcommittee, and we thank you, sir.

Mr. CHABOT. Thank you very much. So it sounds like this administration isn't all that different from some previous administrations, I would note. But in any event, we are both William and Mary graduates and we actually like each other a lot and there ought to be more William and Mary graduates in Congress, I think, don't you?

But in any event, when I first came here two decades ago and after becoming more and more involved on Taiwanese issues, along with Dana Rohrabacher and two Democrats we formed the, we were the founding Members of the Congressional Taiwan Caucus, and it is one of the largest caucuses and I think one of the most important caucuses we have here on Capitol Hill.

But when I first came here, China had a couple hundred missiles aimed directly at Taiwan, now they have 1,600 missiles aimed at Taiwan. I consider myself to be a very good friend of Taiwan, but some constructive criticism that I would give is one of the more frustrating things that I have had. As somebody who is trying to be a friend on Capitol Hill, one of the witnesses—I think it was you, Mr. Blumenthal—who mentioned that the legislature in Taiwan has to get their act together if we are trying to help them militarily to actually have a sufficient budget and then move forward with the budget.

You had different parties involved, you had the DPP and you had, you know, it was a problem. So for years when we were willing to sell them the weapons they couldn't get their act together to buy them, then we had an administration that was less willing to sell the weaponry that they needed.

So I guess my question, and I will go to you, Mr. Blumenthal, since I think you brought it up, how can we finally thread that needle and have the decision makers here who want to supply the weapons, and the Taiwanese leaders who want to purchase those weapons, how do we do that? And then what are the specific things that they need?

I mean obviously it is planes and we were trying for submarines here, but they aren't making anything but nuclear submarines and that is really not what they need. They tried France, and the U.S. doesn't make them anymore, a whole range of things. I think the one I went on that was a World War II-era submarine. We didn't go out on it but we saw what they had available.

I will stop rambling and turn it over to you, Mr. Blumenthal.

Mr. BLUMENTHAL. Sure. I think you are right that we ought not, as good friends of Taiwan, to let them off the hook either. I think 3 percent of GDP is not even enough when you are looking at it. If you look at other national security states facing that kind of threat, from Singapore to South Korea to Israel, 3 percent of GDP is actually paltry.

But there is a chicken and an egg problem, because Taiwan, as painful as it is, Taiwan will buy—it may take a long time—but they will buy everything we put on offer. So in that $30 billion defense package of 2001, the only thing not bought were the submarines, and that was more of the games that we were playing internally because of not wanting to sell diesel submarines for navy reasons.

So what should we be putting on offer to Taiwan? At this point, as you correctly mentioned in terms of the missile threat, the air threat and so much more, things that are survivable, so some kind of submarine program even if they built it themselves in Taiwan. There are licenses sitting in the State Department right now if Taiwan needs to build their own defense that we can offer help with.

Munitions, stand-off munitions of all kinds, UAVs and UCAVs, we have got to think much more creatively and asymmetrically in terms of encouraging shore-based land attack cruise missiles. We have to think much more creatively about what can survive the initial onslaughts since missile defense won't be able to do it anymore. But we ought not let Taiwan off the hook.

Mr. CHABOT. Thank you very much. I appreciate that. Let me, I have got less than a minute to go so let me just touch on a couple of things, and if I had had more time I would have gone into more detail. I am concerned about China using the term "core interest" now with reference to Taiwan. The PRC using that term in reference to Taiwan that is concerning. It is pronounced Hsiao?

Mr. HSIAO. Hsiao.

Mr. CHABOT. Mr. Hsiao, you had kind of raised this issue, and again I don't have time to go into any great detail about it. But with North Korea being as great a threat as it has been for a long time and continues to be maybe even more so now, well, certainly more so now with the development of intercontinental ballistic missiles, and depending on China to help and they have helped virtually nothing up to this point, there is concern that they think they can use Taiwan then as a bargaining chip, and that is something that absolutely cannot happen.

I would strongly urge the relatively new administration not to let that happen because Beijing will say lots of nice things and then actually delivering on them that is a very another thing, and so we should always keep that in mind. And I will certainly, when I talk to the State Department those are the types of things that I will bring to their attention. Thank you very much and I yield back.

Mr. YOHO. Thank you, Mr. Chabot.

Mr. Rohrabacher, you are next.

Mr. ROHRABACHER. Mr. Chairman, I am sorry that I was late. I, actually, you schedule two hearings at the same time you have got to run back and forth and that is what this is.

I have taken a keen interest in Taiwan. During the Cold War, Taiwan's help, especially during the Vietnam War, was instrumental in saving the lives of thousands and thousands of American military personnel. I was not in the military but on my way to Vietnam when I was out of the military I did stop in Taiwan and I was part of an operation that was actually headquartered in Taiwan to try to defeat the communists in Vietnam. That is another lifetime ago.

But let me note today, I think all of these years Taiwan has been a shining example of human rights. That is one of the reasons that the mainland, the gang in the mainland cannot get them out of their mind because they know that this is an example where Chinese people are able to make democracy work and in working for the benefit of the population. I think Beijing is a klepto-dictatorship that is no longer a Marxist-Leninist under anybody's definition of Marx and Lenin.

The people of Taiwan with their free press have been able to maintain a semblance of honest government. I am not saying that they are pure because they are not, we know, but the fact is, Mr. Chairman, Taiwan can show the people of the mainland of China that there is a better way, and thus again are playing a very important role in providing for and ensuring that we will have a peaceful world.

Because unless China in some way reforms out of this clique that is running Beijing—basically the people in Beijing are trying to subjugate their own people and they are ripping them off and they are trying to dominate a huge chunk of the planet—unless they can get down to what democratic government is supposed to be, and that is serving the needs of your own people, there will be a conflict eventually. Taiwan is actually the way that we can send that notice that that will not be permitted.

But I do have a question for you and that is—and I have 2 minutes left. Japan, actually they occupied Taiwan. It was Formosa then for a long time. And how many years was that, decades was that? Was it 100 years? Was it 50 years? What was that? Well, for a significant chunk of history, Formosa was occupied by Japan.

Can Japan play a role now in the security of Taiwan; will that be accepted? Is that something that is too provocative, or would the benefits of that—Japan has not played the role that it should play in the last 50 years because of their penance for World War II. Well, it is time for Japan to start playing a major role again. What should that be in relationship to Taiwan?

Mr. HAMMOND-CHAMBERS. Thank you for the question. I will be very quick and then I will hand it over to Dan and Russell. Certainly on the defense side Japan can discretely partner with Taiwan in the development of domestic capabilities that Taiwan seeks to produce itself. Japan has a robust defense industry community with excellent technologies. I wouldn't expect them to sell a complete platform or system, but they have many technologies that Taiwan could partner with and produce defensive equipment that would help maintain peace and security.

Mr. ROHRABACHER. Very good suggestion.

Mr. BLUMENTHAL. I would say very quickly, a sort of truth in policy is that there is no defense of Japan and the first island chain without Taiwan and Prime Minister Abe certainly knows this and has made for Japan revolutionary changes.

But what we can do—without our leadership it won't go very far. An integrated first island chain strategy on our part would harden the Ryukyu Island chain further than Okinawa, and then have more joint ISR between Taiwan and Japan to be able to track those PLA task forces that are going into the Pacific. That is very much in our interest. Japan has the attitude and aptitude and willingness to do so, but they would need a signal from us. We can really harden that island chain and cause big problems for the PLA Navy.

Mr. HSIAO. I completely agree with everything that was just said. I would just add that it is as much of a political issue as it is a military one and I think that there are significant trends, improvements in terms of how Japan is engaging with Taiwan. For instance, changing its de facto Embassy in Taiwan from the Interchange Association to the Japan-Taiwan Exchange Association to having a senior vice minister visit Taiwan earlier this year.

I think that these trends should be encouraged by the United States and I think the United States can send a strong political signal by upgrading the exchanges between the United States and Taiwan, and the Taiwan Travel Act is one example.

Mr. ROHRABACHER. If there is going to be peace in the world Taiwan and Japan are going to have to play a major role, because I believe China is one of the antagonists we have got to deal with or they will deal with us. Thank you very much.

Mr. YOHO. Thank you, Mr. Rohrabacher. And just in time, it is your turn. I now turn to Mr. Sherman, the ranking member.

Mr. SHERMAN. Mr. Hammond-Chambers, what steps can we take to export more to Taiwan?

Mr. HAMMOND-CHAMBERS. Thank you, Mr. Sherman. I do believe at the core of that question is an expanded trade relationship that would come with some sort of agreement on, again, nomenclature can be played around with of course, but let's for argument's sake call it fair trade agreement. There are a number of areas in which Taiwan——

Mr. SHERMAN. Mr. Hammond.

Mr. HAMMOND-CHAMBERS. Yes, sir.

Mr. SHERMAN. I am looking for approaches that will reduce the trade deficits. So if you are talking about increasing imports as well as increasing exports, do you have a suggestion on how we reduce the trade deficit or reach balanced trade?

Mr. HAMMOND-CHAMBERS. Well, we could certainly sell more weapons to Taiwan. That would reduce the trade deficit. Our defense manufacturers are significant——

Mr. SHERMAN. Many of us have advocated that for national security rather than economic reasons, but——

Mr. HAMMOND-CHAMBERS. You did ask.

Mr. SHERMAN [continuing]. You know, it is—anybody else have any ideas how we would reduce the trade deficit? I see no one else on our witness panel anxious to answer that one. We will move on to the next question which relates to arm sales, but we will address Mr. Blumenthal and Mr. Hsiao.

What are Taiwan's most pressing needs, and I am asking for more of a national security rather than a trade balance answer to this. What are Taiwan's most pressing needs for military hardware? What arms deals to Taiwan do you think the Trump administration would go ahead with, and should we sell them F-35s?

Mr. BLUMENTHAL. We have to look now, given the state of the cross-Strait balance, at things that are survivable, that are dispersible, that are mobile, that can be underwater and still shoot at a landing force, and I think we have to think of things in terms of what China has done to us which is help Taiwan build a A2AD network. So——

Mr. SHERMAN. What network?

Mr. BLUMENTHAL. Anti-access area denial network, the kinds of things that China has done. So China has been able through submarines, through integrated air defense, through integrated C4ISR, through mining, made it very hard for us to operate in places that we used to be able to operate, denying us the space. Those are the kinds of things Taiwan can do.

Mr. SHERMAN. Are there particular weapons systems that would fit that?

Mr. BLUMENTHAL. Submarines, which they want to build in Taiwan but we can have a big component of that, and those are licenses sitting at State right now.

Mr. SHERMAN. What about the F-35?

Mr. BLUMENTHAL. F-35, I would look at many different options just because of the expense. You can do a lot of UAVs and UCAVs, for example, but it is a very expensive platform obviously.

Mr. SHERMAN. How confident would we be that the PRC has not infiltrated somehow Taiwanese defense so that F-35 technology——

Mr. BLUMENTHAL. Well, Taiwan has to do a lot better as do a lot of our allies on security assurance and information assurance.

Mr. SHERMAN. So would you be concerned that if we sold an F-35 that there wouldn't be adequate security?

Mr. BLUMENTHAL. Well, no, because they have broken into our F-35s here and so——

Mr. SHERMAN. They already have the plans.

Mr. BLUMENTHAL [continuing]. They already have what they need.

Mr. SHERMAN. Why don't we go on to Mr. Hsiao.

Mr. HSIAO. Thank you, Ranking Member.

Mr. SHERMAN. You are not brightening up my day, Mr. Blumenthal. Mr. Hsiao.

Mr. HSIAO. On the F-35s I would just say that the Taiwanese military have assessed that they have a need for the F-35s, based on exercises that they have conducted on an annual basis, in order to execute the missions that they assess as necessary in order to deter the People's Liberation Army. I think any assessment on Taiwan's defense needs need to be based at least with a strong consideration of what their defense needs are and what they assess their defense needs are.

I would also add that different sales such as submarines to Taiwan also fill a need on the part of Taiwan to be able to engage China in a manner that targets their weaknesses. So I think it is well known that one of the weaknesses of the PLA is in its ASW, which is anti-submarine warfare, and to be able to have Taiwan be able to possess and be able to operate submarines within the periphery waters would be necessary for the missions that it sees to deter Beijing. And then along with that I would also reinforce Dan and Rupert's comments earlier.

Mr. SHERMAN. Thank you. I see my time has expired.

Mr. YOHO. We will go to Ms. Wagner.

Mrs. WAGNER. Thank you, Mr. Chairman. As we all know, this week, Panama switched diplomatic relations from Taiwan to China. China's checkbook diplomacy is a dangerous provocation to cross-Strait relations, and its cheap tricks in our own backyard are particularly concerning.

I was impressed with President Trump's call to President Tsai Ing-wen, and I am adamant that we fully engage with Taiwan through high level official visits, weapons sales, and pressing for Taiwan's inclusion in international organizations. Taiwan will never be a bargaining chip in U.S.-China relations and we must ensure that the Trump administration provides support to our important democratic partner in the Asia-Pacific.

Mr. Blumenthal, the Trump administration need not alter its support of Taiwan or its outreach to our democratic partners in the country in order to secure China's increased support to counter the North Korean threat. In fact, bowing to China on Taiwan will do no favors for any American policy. How can the new administration prioritize Taiwan's security and democracy even as the President courts President Xi Jinping's collaboration on North Korea?

Mr. BLUMENTHAL. Well, thank you very much for your statement and your question. I think that we have already seen signs that we are not just going to be trying to cozy up and get closer to China because of North Korea. I think patience in the Trump administration is running thin on the North Korea question with respect to China.

I also look at the recent FONOP or challenge, which in some ways was a much more aggressive challenge on the South China Sea than we have done in the past, as a sign that we can walk and chew gum at the same time. Since we are looking for reciprocity with China, China does things we don't like all the time and we still have good relations, we still have cooperative relations with them.

They have militarized, as was mentioned before. They have essentially taken the Paracels, they are gone. They are pretty close to taking the Spratlys if we don't do anything on the Scarborough reef or the Scarborough Shoal. So the idea that China can do all kinds of things we don't like and yet seek our cooperation but we have to cooperate on everything with China is just false.

Then finally on your Panama point I would raise this. We always talk about our policy on both sides of the Strait to maintain the status quo. There is no such thing. China is constantly changing the status quo. Going forward and forcing a country or buying off a country to de-recognize Taiwan is a major change in the status quo. We called Taiwan out on this. We have to call China out on this as well.

Mrs. WAGNER. I agree and it is a provocation.

Mr. Blumenthal and Mr. Hsiao, does the U.S. face unique challenges in China's checkbook diplomacy targeting Central America as opposed to China's efforts earlier this year to obtain diplomatic recognition for—I will try this—Sao Tome and Principe in West Africa?

Mr. HSIAO. Yes, and thank you for that question. To the question on Central America and Beijing's coercive strategy to isolate Taiwan internationally, I think just as Beijing right now is using a multidimensional strategy to isolate Taiwan, I think it is important to have a multidimensional strategy to counter that. I think not only a bilateral mechanism, there needs to be a multilateral mechanism by which the United States can help to enhance Taiwan's international space.

I think in this effort, the Global Cooperation and Training Framework that has been implemented between the United States and Taiwan since 2015 needs to be enhanced, upgraded, and adequately resourced in order to ensure that Taiwan can cooperate with the United States and third-party countries to help overcome this full-court press that I have described as Beijing's strategy to pick off Taiwan's allies and also degrade unofficial relations between Taiwan and other countries.

Mrs. WAGNER. Mr. Blumenthal, any comment?

Mr. BLUMENTHAL. Yeah, very short. I think we have a particular concern with China strategically in Central America without question, but I think China's main motivation around the world is to isolate Taiwan. We should pay special attention to Chinese activities in Central America.

Mrs. WAGNER. I believe my time has run out. Mr. Chairman, I am going to submit the rest of my fantastic questions to this panel——

Mr. YOHO. And they are.

Mrs. WAGNER [continuing]. And they are awfully—for a written response. I thank our witnesses and I thank the chairman.

Mr. YOHO. Thank you, Ann. We will go to Mr. Connolly now from Virginia.

Mr. CONNOLLY. Thank you, Mr. Chairman. It is a pleasure to be here both in my capacity as a member of the committee and subcommittee and also co-chair of the Taiwan Caucus. I have had the privilege of going to Taiwan 23 times since 1988. I was an Eisenhower Fellow and I have seen extraordinary change. When I first went to Taiwan in 1988 it was a one-party state. It was not a functioning democracy and some core freedoms we cherish and so does Taiwan today were not cherished in 1988. There were serious restrictions on speech and political organizing, on dissent and on travel and on investment in the mainland. I have witnessed over that time period one of the greatest changes in a nation I have ever witnessed, and I have traveled a lot.

I wonder, Mr. Hsiao, probably when I first went there you weren't born, but to what would you attribute, and all of you could comment. Why this profound change? I mean what happened in Taiwan? Was it something unique to the people of Taiwan or what was the spark or evolutionary process that led us to this open democratic society in sharp contrast to the other place?

Mr. HSIAO. Thank you for that very profound question, Representative. I think there are two factors. There are internal and external factors. The external factor, I think, is driven by the loss of recognition, the de-recognition by the United States to the PRC

52

that pressured the government from the top down to liberalize, to integrate more Taiwanese into the political process in order to establish a greater foundation for legitimate rule.

And then also at the same time and to give credit to the Taiwanese people who have strove to have a greater freedom and democracy. I think the United States has played a pivotal role in supporting that democratic movement in Taiwan in the '80s and '90s onward. So I would say that it is a confluence of these factors that really drove Taiwan to become the democratic example and model that exists now, to the extent now that it can serve as a model for Southeast Asian countries that are making similar sort of progressions in their political developments.

Mr. CONNOLLY. Mr. Hammond-Chambers, I assume that many of the companies that are members of your Council also operate in the mainland.

Mr. HAMMOND-CHAMBERS. That is correct.

Mr. CONNOLLY. And so how does that work? I mean are they under pressure from Beijing to disinvest in Taiwan or do they turn a blind eye? Do they welcome it? What is that relationship like, what kind of pressure are they under, if any?

Mr. HAMMOND-CHAMBERS. Typically they aren't under any pressure at all. There are several instances where U.S. companies have been identified by PRC authorities in an attempt to be pressured and those typically relate to PRC interpretation of the company overstepping grounds regarding Taiwan sovereignty. So perhaps they might have published something that had Taiwan's official name Republic of China in it, or in some of the instances where some of our larger defense companies have interests in the mainland as well they might have been identified.

I have been the U.S.-Taiwan Business Council for over 20 years. I am not aware of a single instance, however, in which a U.S. company had a long-term impact on its interests in the mainland as a consequence of the fact that it is doing business on Taiwan.

Mr. CONNOLLY. Very interesting. So while Beijing is pressuring the countries like Panama to switch recognition, they are not doing the same in the business side.

Mr. HAMMOND-CHAMBERS. Correct. It is all about the business, Mr. Connolly.

Mr. CONNOLLY. Yeah. Mr. Blumenthal, and by the way you can comment on other things as well, but earlier before this hearing, I know you are aware, we actually approved a bill that for the first time, well, in a long time, has Congress saying enough. We are going to address some issues that we have kind of ceded to the State Department and the White House over many administrations.

I wonder if you might comment on that because one of the things that has concerned me, and wear my other hat in the Taiwan Caucus, is how much at least tacit control we have given to Beijing in terms of the nature of the relationship with Taiwan. We have a statute, the Taiwan Relations Act, which came out of the committee I used to work for that was initiated by Congress and that is the guiding document about the relationship. That document commits us to a certain posture with respect to Taiwan's defense including the sale of defensive weapons.

I don't know that that statute says the President of Taiwan can't come to the United States or to Washington, DC, and yet I remember Presidents of Taiwan calling me kind of on the sly when they were at an airport so we could talk because there was no official visit here. I understand a Presidential Head of State visit is one thing, but I mean putting a bag over your head and pretending you don't exist is quite another.

So I know that is a long question, but I really am bothered by how much power we seem to have ceded Beijing on many facets of the relationship. I am very grateful, Mr. Chairman, that this subcommittee and hopefully the full committee is taking some of that back, finally. But I wanted your comment and then I am done. Thank you.

Mr. BLUMENTHAL. Well, I agree wholeheartedly. I mean, there are many, many factors involved. There is nothing in these communiques, which again are simply joint statements between countries made in the 1980s and 1970s, at a very different time that says anything about who our President can call or speak to or visit or meet. That is somehow a mystical paper in the State Department, somewhere that was written probably 30, 40 years ago, somebody interpreting what we meant by those communiques. We may be stuck with those communiques in the One China Policy, but we are certainly not stuck with China telling us whom we can meet with. It is so very much in our interests, and in their interests that we keep an ongoing high level dialogue with Taiwan for the sake of predictability and stability.

I would finally say that one thing that a lot of people are looking at now is the level of Chinese propaganda and political warfare the Chinese Communist Party targeted against the United States. It is much different than Russia or other rivals, but it is a huge problem and it has changed the minds of many people.

They have convinced many important people including probably policy makers that the communiques say something that they don't, that we acknowledge that Taiwan is part of China. We do not. We leave the status to be determined by the two parties. They have made great headway and it is an active political warfare campaign. It is not just passive diplomacy or neglect.

Mr. CONNOLLY. Thank you. And Mr. Chairman, thank you.

Mr. YOHO. Mr. Connolly, I would like to work on some of this stuff to draft policies that we can direct maybe the State Department or the administration.

We are going to, if you guys have enough time I would like to go back to Ranking Member Sherman and then I would like to end with a couple statements.

Mr. SHERMAN. Mr. Hammond-Chambers, we have had this description of how China is on the international stage trying to hem in, delegitimize Taiwan, but I wonder how that squares with their economic behavior. Can you describe cross-Strait investment and cross-Strait trade over the last few years?

Mr. HAMMOND-CHAMBERS. Yes, Mr. Sherman, it continues to expand quite frankly. The economic links between the two sides remain robust, somewhat cooled down since Tsai Ing-wen took over. But for the most part——

Mr. SHERMAN. How big is the investment of each country in assets in the other——

Mr. HAMMOND-CHAMBERS. The PRC investment in China is tightly held, so very minimal.

Mr. SHERMAN. PRC investment in Taiwan?

Mr. HAMMOND-CHAMBERS. In Taiwan is minimal. There are some areas that the PRC could invest in but it is quite tightly held now. Conversely, in China, Taiwan investment is massive and a lot of it has circumvented regular ways to monitor, so I have seen numbers ranging from $100 to $250 billion worth of Taiwan capital invested in China.

Mr. SHERMAN. And what do we do to persuade the Taiwanese that putting their investments in a country that may seize them at any moment may not be as desirable as investing in the 30th Congressional District of California?

Mr. HAMMOND-CHAMBERS. Well, I think there are many Taiwanese who would like to do nothing more than invest $250 billion in your district, sir, but I——

Mr. SHERMAN. One billion at a time.

Mr. HAMMOND-CHAMBERS. Okay. But there are many people in Taiwan including the present Taiwan administration that have deep concerns about what has transpired over the last 20 years and have policies such as the Southbound Policy to try and curb that. However, they have limited control over their businesses in this regard who have less of an interest in the national security concerns.

Mr. SHERMAN. They have a lot of control if they choose to pass laws, and if they choose to simply do what is politically popular with the economically important then they have no power. The idea of creating what could be as high as a $250 billion investment in Beijing creates powerful forces in Taipei to lobby for the Beijing position.

A failure of a business to conduct such lobbying could impair the value of their investment or cause their investment assets to decline in yield or to be treated as favorably. The prospect of the seizure of those investments should there be some sort of crisis means that you have very powerful economic interests that may want to reunify on any basis that protects those investments. But again the opportunities in the 30th congressional district are still available. I will go to the other witnesses. And also in Florida there is some excellent——

Mr. YOHO. I am glad you added us in there because your side—no offense—you are promoting that and she is promoting the casinos. I am like we need to throw Florida in there.

Mr. SHERMAN. We will throw Florida in there a little bit, but once they see the opportunities in the 30th district—let's see. How can and in what cases is China, well, I guess in every case China has tried to keep Taiwan out of international organizations. So the question is, really, is how can Congress help resist such pressure and what can we do to assist Taiwan in joining all the international organizations from the World Health Organization to Civil Aviation to U.N. Framework on Climate Change, Interpol, et cetera? Mr. Blumenthal, then Mr. Hsiao.

Mr. BLUMENTHAL. Well, we already very much have the international legal basis to do so because of the WTO accession and Taiwan's accession into it. So all the arguments that China makes against Taiwan's membership particularly in organizations that don't require statehood, or a recognition of statehood, are very specious because they agree to the WTO accession already.

Mr. SHERMAN. And does WTO require statehood?

Mr. BLUMENTHAL. We negotiated in a way that didn't and so we have the basis now, the diplomatic and legal framework to negotiate Taiwan's accession to any international organization that doesn't require statehood.

Mr. SHERMAN. So why does China work so hard in their effort to delegitimize the sovereignty of Taiwan to keep Taiwan out of organizations' membership in which does not establish sovereignty?

Mr. BLUMENTHAL. Because there is very little pushback. So for example, we can have an FTA—we have the basis of an FTA in international law and diplomatic custom.

Mr. SHERMAN. You are saying FTA or DA?

Mr. BLUMENTHAL. Yeah, I know. I don't mean to talk about the trade deficit. We could theoretically have a free trade agreement, but China pushes back by saying that that would confer statehood upon Taiwan, a completely specious argument given——

Mr. SHERMAN. Especially if the agreement provided for a reduction in the trade deficit. Let me go on to Mr. Hsiao. What can Congress do to help Taiwan get into these international organizations?

Mr. HSIAO. Thank you, Ranking Member. I would just add that I do think there needs to be a more inclusive approach in dealing with Taiwan's international space and how the United States strategize its approach to getting Taiwan into international organizations. I would add that I think there is a good existing mechanism through the Global Cooperation and Training Framework, and I think that it can be expanded to lead as an example of how Taiwan and the United States can cooperate with third-party countries in trying to in areas of health alleviation, in areas of women empowerment, in democratization, energy, that these are functional areas of cooperation where people will see, other countries will see the value of Taiwan's contribution, and any efforts on the part of the PRC to limit that would just fly in the face of decency of what is necessary for as Taiwan as a contributing member of the international community.

Mr. SHERMAN. I yield back.

Mr. YOHO. Thank you. If you will indulge me just for a few more minutes, what I have gained and what I have deemed out of this is we see an aggressive China. We see that they are continuing this. We are seeing they are putting more pressure on the international community to exclude Taiwan as a semi-independent state of their own, a democracy that has been very successful, very fruitful, and we keep hearing that we need to partner with China. I think China needs to partner with us and the rest of the free world.

I say that when we look at our trade, the last report I had China borrowed, stole, or highjacked over $600 billion of intellectual property. I don't want a partner like that. We need to put more pressure—and like you said, Mr. Blumenthal, the reason they are doing what they are, nobody is standing up. It is time to stand up because we see the writing on the wall. If we don't do it now, it will be easier to do it now than to wait another 5 years because Taiwan will be that much more isolated. The South China Sea will also be that much more boxed in, and then the trade that we talk about and the spread of democracy of our tenth largest trading partner, it will affect us.

So coming out of this meeting I always like to have action items. When I read the USTR's recommends that the Trump administration end the policy of packaging and return to a regularized process, whereby Taiwan would be treated like other security assistance partners all the way from the U.S. accepting letters of request for pricing and availability data to consulting with notifying Congress of an intention to sell arms to Taiwan. We have put it into this quagmire or this box where, yeah, we are doing it but we are kind of hiding it so we don't want to offend anybody. I think we need to go back to be bold and just say yeah, we are, because it is in the 1979 agreement.

We have also, as an action item we put in a free trade agreement that we entered as House Resolution 271 in April 6th of 2017. I think there is still time for you to get on that even in the 33rd district of California.

Mr. SHERMAN. Yeah, as long as we add a provision about requiring a system to reach balanced trade I will be on it.

Mr. YOHO. I want to touch base on that right now as a little aside on the trade deficit. It remains large, but Taiwan has imported larger and larger percentage of imports from the U.S. over recent years, and by a percentage our deficit has been cut in half over those years and we are going in the right way.

But as far as more action items and I think you heard a resounding theme in here and I agree wholeheartedly with this, and that theme is Taiwan will not be used as a bargaining chip and I think China needs to understand that from this point forward. I think we will stand real strong and we will get the rest of the countries to do that too.

You know, the freedom of navigation, we need to do more of those because China has created on their islands, according to their Ambassador that I talked to, lighthouses on the Spratly Islands strictly for peaceful navigational purposes. I agree, and I think we should all utilize that and thank them for that.

The free trade agreement, like I said, we introduced on April 6th, and letters of support for the importance of the contributions of the health, worldwide health organizations that Taiwan has contributed to, and we are sending letters to support their inclusion in these organizations, and we haven't had a communique since 1982.

When you read those it is kind of like your parents, well, yeah, you can go ahead and do that but don't tell your mom or don't tell anybody you are doing that. I mean that is the way I read those and I think we need to come out, maybe it is time for a fourth one that has clarity and purpose so that we can go into the 21st century with a clear direction, a peaceful direction, and it is time that we as the United States showed the leadership in that.

Do you guys have anything that you want to end up with, maybe 30 seconds apiece? Mr. Hammond-Chambers?

Mr. HAMMOND-CHAMBERS. Yes, just very quickly, Mr. Chairman, I would just like to point out on my colleague's point about information warfare, we had this week we had the switch in recognition from Panama. One of the challenges that we face is that the PRC continues to define what our One China Policy is.

Mr. YOHO. Exactly.

Mr. HAMMOND-CHAMBERS. And it does real, real damage. I understand Mr. Tillerson was up on the Hill yesterday. He said the One China Policy. I commend you in saying our One China Policy, because what the Chinese like to do is they like to define our One China Policy as their One China Principle. And regrettably, all too often it shows up in our media.

Mr. YOHO. Right.

Mr. HAMMOND-CHAMBERS. Two days ago, USA Today, yesterday, the Washington Post and the Associated Press, the Chinese definition of the One China Principle as our One China Policy, so I would certainly encourage you and your committee members, sir, when you have an opportunity to be very clear about U.S. policy on that standpoint.

Mr. YOHO. Thank you.

Mr. Blumenthal?

Mr. BLUMENTHAL. Yeah, I agree with all of your suggestions. I would include in that getting the State Department, Defense Department, and intelligence agencies to report on China's active information warfare, political warfare against us in a——

Mr. YOHO. Stay tuned, we have a good bill coming out on that.

Mr. BLUMENTHAL. Good. You know what, I am not as smart as you guys. You are ahead of me.

Mr. YOHO. It is the guys behind me.

Mr. BLUMENTHAL. But I would caution against a fourth communique because I think that doesn't include Taiwan and the Chinese have gotten the better end of the stick on the last three.

Mr. YOHO. I intend to have it written to where it, you know, I don't want to say make America great or put America first, but the only way you can do that is if you help your partners you are dealing with become very successful too.

Mr. BLUMENTHAL. Right. The greater point I was making is that we have no other policy, just based on joint statements made in the Cold War and it is ridiculous.

Mr. YOHO. It is. It is absolutely ridiculous.

Mr. BLUMENTHAL. It does not reflect——

Mr. YOHO. In the 21st century with superpowers.

Mr. BLUMENTHAL. That is right. It doesn't reflect the geopolitical moment anymore.

Mr. SHERMAN. I would add one other thing. There is an Article I to the United States Constitution. It provides for the ratification of treaties. Nothing that you are describing, a press release from a President no longer living is not binding on the people of the United States. The Vienna Convention on the Law of Treaties, you have got ratified treaty, you have got legislative executive agreement, unratified treaty, and then you have got press releases from no longer living Presidents.

Let me put this another way. A ratified treaty is like a minister, a groom, a bride, rings. This communique is like five margaritas at a seedy singles bar——

Mr. YOHO. In California.

Mr. SHERMAN [continuing]. In California. And let me tell the chairman that certainly five margaritas at a seedy singles bar in California is not a binding commitment. Thank God.

Mr. YOHO. Mr. Hsiao, do you have something you want to end up with?

Mr. HSIAO. Thank you, Chairman. Thank you, Ranking Member. I think I would just like to close on the need for a greater clarity on U.S. defense commitments to Taiwan. I say this with sincerity, that the massive military buildup across the Strait and China's continued refusal to renounce the use of force against Taiwan is a threat to the peace and security of the Western Pacific area.

While the United States had managed to deter Beijing from taking destructive military action against Taiwan in the last four decades, I think when China was relatively weak, and I go to the point that you have made, the premise of China saying that it was weak then it is stronger now, that we are approaching dangerously close to where the benefits of this, the cost outweighs the benefits.

So I think as the PLA grows stronger, a perceived lack of commitment by the United States to defend Taiwan will further embolden Beijing to use force to resolve the Taiwan issue. Thank you.

Mr. YOHO. I think that was very well spoken by all of you, and I thank you for wrapping it up that way. I liked the levity of it. I didn't know you had so much levity. That is good to know. But I appreciate your thoughts, your expertise, and what you do, and we will move forward with some of the suggestions you had. Reconsider the fourth communique and maybe consult you before we go forward.

That pretty much concludes this hearing and we thank everybody for participating. We thank the crowd for being here. You guys were great to stay here the whole time in this hot room. This committee hearing is adjourned.

[Whereupon, at 4:20 p.m., the subcommittee was adjourned.]

APPENDIX

MATERIAL SUBMITTED FOR THE RECORD

SUBCOMMITTEE HEARING NOTICE
COMMITTEE ON FOREIGN AFFAIRS
U.S. HOUSE OF REPRESENTATIVES
WASHINGTON, DC 20515-6128

Subcommittee on Asia and the Pacific
Ted Yoho (R-FL), Chairman

June 15, 2017

TO: MEMBERS OF THE COMMITTEE ON FOREIGN AFFAIRS

You are respectfully requested to attend an OPEN hearing of the Committee on Foreign Affairs, to be held by the Subcommittee on Asia and the Pacific in Room 2200 of the Rayburn House Office Building (and available live on the Committee website at http://www.ForeignAffairs.house.gov):

DATE: Thursday, June 15, 2017

TIME: 2:45 p.m.

SUBJECT: Renewing Assurances: Strengthening U.S.-Taiwan Ties

WITNESSES: Mr. Rupert J. Hammond-Chambers
                     President
                     U.S.-Taiwan Business Council

                     Mr. Dan Blumenthal
                     Director of Asian Studies and Resident Fellow
                     American Enterprise Institute

                     Mr. Russell Hsiao
                     Executive Director
                     Global Taiwan Institute

By Direction of the Chairman

The Committee on Foreign Affairs seeks to make its facilities accessible to persons with disabilities. If you are in need of special accommodations, please call 202/225-5021 at least four business days in advance of the event, whenever practicable. Questions with regard to special accommodations in general (including availability of Committee materials in alternative formats and assistive listening devices) may be directed to the Committee.

COMMITTEE ON FOREIGN AFFAIRS

MINUTES OF SUBCOMMITTEE ON _____ *Subcommittee on Asia and the Pacific* _____ HEARING

Day **Thursday** Date **June 15, 2017** Room **2200 RHOB**

Starting Time **2:50pm** Ending Time **4:20pm**

Recesses _____ (_____ to _____)(_____ to _____)(_____ to _____)(_____ to _____)(_____ to _____)(_____ to _____)

Presiding Member(s)

Rep. Ted Yoho

Check all of the following that apply:

Open Session ☑
Executive (closed) Session ☐
Televised ☐

Electronically Recorded (taped) ☐
Stenographic Record ☐

TITLE OF HEARING:

"Renewing Assurances: Strengthening U.S.-Taiwan Ties"

SUBCOMMITTEE MEMBERS PRESENT:

*Rep. Ted Yoho, Rep Steve Chabot, Rep. Dana Rohrabacher, Rep. Ann Wagner
Rep. Brad Sherman, Rep. Ami Bera, Rep. Gerald Connolly, Rep. Dina Titus*

NON-SUBCOMMITTEE MEMBERS PRESENT: *(Mark with an * if they are not members of full committee.)*

Rep. Ed Royce

HEARING WITNESSES: Same as meeting notice attached? Yes ☑ No ☐
(If "no", please list below and include title, agency, department, or organization.)

STATEMENTS FOR THE RECORD: *(List any statements submitted for the record.)*

Rep. Wagner QFR

TIME SCHEDULED TO RECONVENE _____
or
TIME ADJOURNED _____

Subcommittee Staff Associate

<u>Statement and Questions for the Record</u>
Congresswoman Ann Wagner
"Renewing Assurances: Strengthening U.S.-Taiwan Ties"
June 15, 2017

Thank you, Mr. Chairman, for organizing this hearing. As we all know, this week, Panama switched diplomatic relations from Taiwan to China. China's checkbook diplomacy is a dangerous provocation to cross-strait relations, and its cheap tricks in our own backyard are particularly concerning. I was impressed with President Trump's call to President Tsai Ing-wen, and I am adamant that we fully engage with Taiwan through high-level official visits, weapons sales, and pressing for Taiwan's inclusion in international organizations. Taiwan will never be a bargaining chip in U.S.-China relations, and we must ensure that the Trump Administration provides support to our important democratic partner in the Asia-Pacific.

1. Mr. Blumenthal, the Trump Administration need not alter its support of Taiwan or its outreach to our democratic partners in the country in order to secure China's increased support to counter the North Korean threat. In fact, bowing to China on Taiwan will do no favors for any American policy. How can the new Administration prioritize Taiwan's security and democracy even as the President courts Xi Jinping's collaboration on North Korea?

2. Mr. Blumenthal and Mr. Hsiao, does the U.S. face unique challenges in China's checkbook diplomacy targeting Central America? (As opposed to China's efforts earlier this year to obtain diplomatic recognition from Sao Tome and Principe in West Africa.)

   Mr. Hsiao's Response: The PRC's checkbook diplomacy into Central America presents an unique challenge for the United States in the sense that the region is the United States' backyard. Beijing's establishment of diplomatic relations with Panama is a signal of China's growing influence in the region. While the PRC's checkbook diplomacy bears directly on Taiwan's diplomatic space, it also has an indirect and significant impact on the United States' strategic interests. Although China's motive in the region has been primarily commercial, the Panama case demonstrates that its interests extend beyond purely commercial matters and could be seen as an effort to balance against U.S. longstanding ties with its Asian allies and partners.

3. Mr. Hammond-Chambers, Taiwan has rolled out a new economic strategy that focuses on increasing ties with ASEAN and South Asia. How can the government help Taiwanese companies shift corporate strategy away from China and into new markets?

   Mr. Hammond Chambers' Response: The New Southbound Policy (NSP) is intended to expand both bilateral trade and mutual investment between Taiwan and 18 countries in Southeast Asia, South Asia and Australasia, with a particular focus on people-to-people ties and on developing entrepreneurships and encouraging startups. The Taiwan government could take a number of steps to incentivize its domestic companies to pursue business with these countries, rather than continuing to focus on China:

   - Providing tax credits and other incentives to Taiwan businesses that

source materials or labor from NSP countries
- Developing loan and grant programs for Taiwan businesses that make new investments in NSP countries
- Directing state-owned enterprises to focus their business priorities on NSP countries
- Enacting government contracting standards that prioritize businesses embracing the NSP
- Negotiating additional bilateral (or multilateral) trade agreements with NSP countries, to encourage expanded trade ties (Taiwan already has trade agreements with several countries covered under the policy, including New Zealand and Singapore.)
- Unilaterally reducing trade barriers and relaxing trade restrictions for NSP countries, to encourage the free flow of goods and services
- Focusing its NSP efforts on specific sectors where included countries are clamoring for investment (e.g. infrastructure, where India has expressed its interest in receiving foreign investment)
- Making further efforts to cooperate with the NSP countries on specific issue areas of mutual concern, in order to open additional markets for Taiwan companies. (e.g. Taiwan's recent initiatives to provide medical assistance and agricultural technology)
- Continuing efforts to sponsor business matching events for NSP countries, and continuing to aid Taiwan companies in setting up distribution outlets through the region

4. Mr. Hsiao, earlier this year, China released nine Singaporean armored transport vehicles after holding them in Hong Kong for two months in retaliation for Singapore's military relationship with Taiwan. Can we expect China to continue to take such action against Singapore and others in the future if cross-strait tensions remain high?

Mr. Hsiao's Response: Beijing's strategy is to coerce Taiwan's leaders into accepting its terms for negotiation on unification by dividing Taiwan internally and isolating it internationally. The PRC has been utilizing its considerable economic, diplomatic, and military clout, especially over smaller but key non-diplomatic partners of Taiwan to prevent them from engaging with Taipei in ways that it considers to run afoul of its "One China" principle. It is also using these means to express its opposition to the Taiwan government's approach to cross-Strait relations. Indeed, the PRC has insisted that Taiwan accepts the so-called "1992 consensus," which the Tsai administration has resisted in explicitly affirming despite her commitment to adhere to the ROC constitution, Act Governing Relations between the People of the Taiwan Area and the Mainland Area, and the historical fact of the 1992 meetings and subsequent understandings. Beijing's efforts to pressure Singapore is as an attempt to broaden the application of its "One China" principle, and pressure countries with significant political, economic, and military ties with Taipei to conform to its preferred definition of cross-Strait relations. The case of Singapore will not likely be an isolated example.

5. Mr. Blumenthal, in addition to or alongside a Free Trade Agreement, what can the United States do to increase economic engagement with Taiwan under the Trump Administration?